Software Engineering Risk Management
Finding Your Path Through the Jungle

Reference Guide — Version 1.0 for Windows®95

T0256918

Information in this guide is subject to change. The software application described in this guide is furnished under a license agreement. The software may be used or copied only in accordance with the terms of the agreement. No part of this guide may be reproduced or transmitted in any form or by any means, electronic or mechanical, including photocopying and recording, for any purpose without the express written permission of LearnerFirst, Inc.

Trademark Acknowledgments LearnerFirst is a registered trademark of LearnerFirst, Incorporated. Names of products mentioned herein are used for identification purposes only and may be trademarks and/or registered trademarks of their respective companies.

License Agreement LearnerFirst, Inc. provides the software application and documentation under the following conditions:
- The customer agrees that all techniques, algorithms, and processes contained in LearnerFirst, Inc.'s products and programs or any extraction thereof constitute trade secrets of LearnerFirst, Inc. and shall be safeguarded by the customer.
- The customer shall not copy, reproduce, remanufacture, or in any way duplicate all or part of LearnerFirst, Inc.'s products or documentation. Personal software backups are allowed.
- The customer assumes all responsibility for any loss or corruption of data or programs.

Limited Warranty LearnerFirst, Inc. warrants the CD on which the software is provided to be free from defects in materials and workmanship, under normal use, for a period of ninety (90) days from the date of delivery. LearnerFirst, Inc.'s only liability shall be the replacement of any defective CD if the original CD is returned to LearnerFirst, Inc.

LearnerFirst makes no warranty of any kind with regard to this guide, including, but not limited to, the implied warranties as to merchantability and fitness for any particular purpose. The entire risk as to the quality and performance of the products and programs lies with the customer. In no event is LearnerFirst, Inc. liable to the customer for any damages arising from the use, misuse, or inability to use this product.

Software Engineering Risk Management
Finding Your Path Through the Jungle

Reference Guide — Version 1.0 for Windows®95

Dale Walter Karolak

LearnerFirst ®
IEEE Computer Society

A product of Knowledge Harvesting™ from LearnerFirst
Created especially for the IEEE Computer Society

LearnerFirst.

Los Alamitos, California

Washington   ●   Brussels   ●   Tokyo

Library of Congress Cataloging-in-Publication Data

Karolak, Dale Walter.
    Software engineering risk management: finding your path through
the jungle / Dale Walter Karolak.
      p. cm.
    ISBN 0-8186-7970-0
    1. Software engineering.   2. Risk management.   I. Title.
QA76.758.K35   1998
005.1—dc21
                              98-10446
                              CIP

IEEE Computer Society Press Order Number SW07970
Library of Congress Number 98-10446
ISBN 0-8186-7970-0

Additional copies may be ordered from:

IEEE Computer Society Press	IEEE Service Center	IEEE Computer Society	IEEE Computer Society
Customer Service Center	445 Hoes Lane	13, Avenue de l'Aquilon	Ooshima Building
10662 Los Vaqueros Circle	P.O. Box 1331	B-1200 Brussels	2-19-1 Minami-Aoyama
P.O. Box 3014	Piscataway, NJ 08855-1331	BELGIUM	Minato-ku, Tokyo 107
Los Alamitos, CA 90720-1314	Tel: +1-908-981-1393	Tel: +32-2-770-2198	JAPAN
Tel: +1-714-821-8380	Fax: +1-908-981-9667	Fax: +32-2-770-8505	Tel: +81-3-3408-3118
Fax: +1-714-821-4641	mis.custserv@computer.org	euro.ofc@computer.org	Fax: +81-3-3408-3553
Email: cs.books@computer.org			tokyo.ofc@computer.org

IEEE Computer Society
Publisher: Matt Loeb
Developmental Editor: Cheryl Baltes
Advertising/Promotions: Tom Fink
Production Editor: Lisa O'Conner

LearnerFirst, Inc.
President: Larry Todd Wilson
Knowledge Engineer: Jarick Rager
Knowledge Engineer: Pam Daugherty
Programming Consultant: Jeff Spears
Artist: Jenny Kimbrell

Printed in the United States of America

Contents

INTRODUCING SERIM: Software Engineering Risk Management

Welcome! The purpose of this Reference Guide is to provide you with the detailed information you will need to master the basic functions and content of the Software Engineering Risk Management (SERIM) application.

This software application is designed to lead you through each step in the software risk management process, from beginning to end. A custom database within the application organizes, saves, and manages your data, thus minimizing the work related to analysis and implementation. You save time by learning, doing, and documenting at the same time!

Achieving the Best Results

1. Concentrate on one step at a time.
   The software application is organized according to the steps in the software risk management process. It is divided into modules, and steps within each module. As you work through the application, focus only on the step at hand. The application leads you through each step, one at a time, so you do not have to be concerned about keeping up with information that was recently entered. The application captures all of your typed-in responses in a database. When your previous responses are needed at certain points in the application, they will be recalled and presented to you, so that you can perform a step. As you work through the steps in a process, we suggest that you go through all the steps in order.

2. Use this application as part of your work routine.
   We suggest that you strive to use this application as part of your normal work routine. To facilitate this integration, you may prefer to install the software application on a personal computer (PC) in your work setting. You can then access the software application whenever you need assistance or want to work on a particular process.

   The software application can also be used in group or team settings. For example, set up a PC in a conference room, and use the application as a facilitator to guide discussions. If the application is used in a team setting, please abide by the terms of the licensing agreement that specifies one copy per licensee.

3. Dedicate at least 20 minutes each time you use the application. If you are working individually, try to dedicate at least 20 minutes or more for each work session. The application is designed so that you can accomplish a significant part of your work within 20 minutes.

4. Consider different ways to use the software application.
   - Systematically work through each of the modules and steps, in the order of presentation.
   - Print out reports and discuss the contents with co-workers.
   - Return to particular steps when you want to remember how decisions were made, or review how data was collected.

Tips for Application Use in a Team Setting

A group or team meeting may provide a good setting for the software engineering risk management process. Consider holding group/team discussions in a conference room equipped with a laptop computer, overhead projector, and LCD plate or other projection device.

Load the software application on the laptop computer. Appoint a team recorder to enter the team's responses to the questions that are asked in each step. Use the steps in the application to help keep the team focused on the tasks to be accomplished and facilitate group decision-making.

Other materials that may be needed for a team meeting include:

Additional Chairs	Easel with Flip Chart	Extension Cord
LCD Projection Panel	Marker Board	Markers
Masking Tape	Name Tags	Overhead Projector
Pens, Pencils	Laptop PC	PC Monitor
Screen	Transparencies	

Common Characteristics of Each Step

Each step contains support information and guidance. The support information will improve your understanding of the software risk management process. The guidance will help you–step by step– accomplish a particular task.

A step may contain up to three different types of support information, which can be found in the application's Smart Help System™.

- **Description** - A description provides an introduction to the step, as well as detailed procedural guidance about how to perform the step. It will include information about inputs, outputs, and required resources.
- **Purpose** - The purpose communicates the aim or the goal of the step. "Why should I perform this step?"
- **Example** - An example provides contextual (conditional) knowledge that tells "when" something works and "why" one approach works better than another. The example may be a story, or information from the author's real-life experiences.

How to Use the Application

The Software Engineering Risk Management (SERIM) application contains three modules:

- **Project Description**
- **Project Assessment**
- **Analytical Perspectives**

The first screen you will see is the Welcome Screen. From this screen you can click on INTRO to read more information about navigating within the application, or click on the picture of the explorer to go directly to the Project Description Module. **NOTE**: After your initial entry into the application, you can click on the box at the bottom, left corner of the screen to turn off the Welcome Screen. If you select this option, the Welcome Screen will no longer appear when you enter the application.

To begin working through the application, go to the Main Screen, and click on the explorer holding the lantern. This will take you to the

Project Description module. Within this module, you will enter some basic identifying information about your project. When you have completed your data entry, return to the Main Screen and click on the explorer reading the map to go to the next module, Project Assessment.

In the Project Assessment module, you will assign ratings on a scale of 0 to 10 ("*" for not applicable) to a series of metric questions within ten categories of risk factors. You will need to complete the Project Description and Project Assessment modules before proceeding to the Analytical Perspectives, so that the application can use your assessment ratings to calculate your project's risk scores.

When you have completed your Project Assessment, return to the Main Screen and choose any of the five Analytical Perspectives to analyze your project's risk scores.

Choosing an Analytical Perspective provides you with a way to look at your project's risks from any or all of five different points of view. Analyzing your project's risks from five different points of view will enable you to focus on your highest priority risk areas and metric questions, and to create action plans to increase your project's potential for success.

How, then, can you recognize risk areas or metric questions that are high priority? Consider the following points as you "drill down" through the levels in any of the five analytical perspectives to the individual metric questions. The presence of one or more of these conditions should alert you to the need to develop an action plan to resolve issues and problems.
1.   An individual low score (below 5)
2.   A significant drop in score
1.   A downward trend in scores, even if current score is above 5

To choose an Analytical Perspective, click on the animal representing the desired perspective. You can work through any or all of the perspectives, in any order you choose. As you work through each analytical perspective, you will be able to create an action plan to raise the score of any individual metric question. The five perspectives are:
•   **Risk Factors** – From this perspective you will analyze how each of the ten risk factors impacts your project.

- **Risk Elements** – From this perspective, you will analyze the data from your assessment of the 10 risk factors as they impact Technical Risks, Cost Risks, and Schedule Risks.
- **Risk Categories** – From this perspective, you will analyze the data from your assessment of the 10 risk factors as they impact the Software Development Process and the Software Product.
- **Risk Activities** – From this perspective, you will analyze the data from your assessment of the 10 risk factors as they impact Risk Identification, Risk Strategy and Planning, Risk Assessment, Risk Mitigation and Avoidance, Risk Reporting, and Risk Prediction. (Within each activity, risks are considered from the operational, strategic, technical, business, industry, and practitioner points of view.)
- **Development Phases** – From this perspective, you will analyze the data from your assessment of the 10 risk factors as they impact each phase of the software development cycle: Pre-Requirements, Requirements, Design, Coding, Testing, and Delivery and Maintenance.

To illustrate the application of the SERIM methodology in simulated situations, three sample projects are included within this Software Engineering Risk Management application.

Example 1 - Satellite Software
Example 2 - PC Project
Example 3 - Embedded Project

Detailed information about these examples can be found in the section of this Reference Guide entitled "**WORKING WITH SERIM: Examples.**"

A Message from the Author

Welcome to Software Engineering Risk Management (SERIM). As a professional associated with the development of software, you are well aware that the software development process can truly be a jungle, filled with hazards that lie in wait to sabotage your projects. These hazards (risks) are numerous, and often complex.

The purpose of this application is to help you find a safer path through this jungle by assessing risk factors, analyzing risks from several different perspectives, and developing focused action plans to manage risks *before* they sabotage your projects. I have used the mathematics of probability to design the formulas that will help you assess and manage risks in the complex software development environment. Complete information on the SERIM Model's equations is included in the software application and in this Reference Guide.

You can use the SERIM application to monitor risks at any point in the development cycle. You can perform your SERIM assessments on a regular schedule for each project, or as indicated by your own observations. Or you can combine these two strategies to manage risks as your projects develop. Whatever strategy you choose, the SERIM approach will help you find a safer path through the jungle!

I wish you success in using this application to manage risks for your software projects.

With best regards from a fellow explorer,

Dale Karolak

About the Author

Dr. Dale Walter Karolak

Dr. Karolak is currently an Engineering Director at TRW Automotive Electronics. His previous positions include Software and System Engineering Manager at ITT Aerospace / Communications, and Software Engineer at GTE Communications Systems R&D Labs. He received his Ph.D. in Software Engineering from The Union Institute in Cincinnati, Ohio, his M.B.A. from the University of Phoenix, and his B.S. in Computer Science from Central Michigan University.

Dr. Karolak is the author of the IEEE's best selling book, ***Software Engineering Risk Management***. He has presented and published over 10 papers in the areas of software management, metrics, reliability, quality, testing, and architecture at IEEE, ACM, NSIA, Association of Management, Applied Software Measurement, International Software Engineering Research Forum, and Medical Device conferences and journals. He also holds a patent on "Communication Management System Architecture," and has three other software architecture and communication patents pending. He is a member of the IEEE, ACM and SAE societies.

About LearnerFirst

Since its incorporation in 1992, LearnerFirst has focused on creating revolutionary learning and performance resources. We have invented many pioneering technologies and have evolved world-class processes in the knowledge management domain. One of LearnerFirst's most advanced capabilities is Knowledge Harvesting™, the process that was used to create this software application. The Harvesting process involves:

- eliciting (capturing) a content expert's knowledge, by using structured interviews.
- formalizing (organizing and structuring) the content expert's knowledge.
- designing software and other learning support media, so that this knowledge can be shared and easily applied by anyone who works in the expert's content area.

LearnerFirst's software development process is built on a valid, comprehensive philosophical and theoretical foundation, and offers:

- unsurpassed production capability. (LearnerFirst can create software and other learning support media in a fraction of the time required by competitive knowledge engineering approaches and authoring toolkits.)
- consistent process and outcome.
- streamlined software programming and debugging.
- the ability to make improvements quickly and easily.

The **mission** of LearnerFirst is to individualize the process of managing personal and organizational knowledge. We believe that learning is ultimately the personal journey of each individual learner in a community, and that individualized learning support is the highest goal of education.

Our **vision** is to provide knowledge management tools and an infrastructure that supports a way of life in which everyone can access extensive individualized know-how for personal and community gain.

About The IEEE Computer Society

The IEEE Computer Society celebrated its 50th anniversary in 1996. This significant milestone was achieved thanks to the active involvement of our membership. The growth of the society and our industry is truly astounding. In the 1950's our membership was less than 10,000. Our international reach began in the late 1960's, and we currently represent more than 90,000 members worldwide. Today we truly are the world's Computer Society.

The Computer Society's vision is to become the leading provider of technical information and services to the world's computing professionals. Headquartered in Washington, DC, the society serves its members from offices in California, Tokyo, and Brussels. The society is the largest technical society within the Institute of Electrical and Electronics Engineers (IEEE).

INSTALLING SERIM

The installation program (setup.exe) will install **Software Engineering Risk Management** on your computer. The installation program will decompress the application files from the CD, copy them to the location specified on your hard disk, and configure the Windows®95 operating system and the application for your needs. The installation process will take about 10 minutes. By necessity, the installation program will make at least one entry in your system registry file.

You can uninstall the entire application at any time by following the UNINSTALLING SERIM instructions. The application will be removed from your system, leaving as few traces as possible.

Important! The installation instructions must be followed precisely in order to use the UNINSTALLING SERIM procedure. **NOTE**: The images you see on your computer screen may look somewhat different from the pictures included in this manual, due to differences in computer settings and configurations.

First, check your computer's characteristics. To run the SERIM application on your computer, you need:
- Pentium 66 MHz processor (minimum)
- 16 MB of random access memory (RAM) or more
- 30 MB free disk space (installation may require more space)
- Microsoft Windows®95
- A CD-ROM drive (for installation)
- A Super VGA (SVGA) graphics adapter card capable of displaying at least 256 colors at 640 X 480 pixel resolution
- Windows-compatible mouse or other pointing device

Then install the application. When you install the application, the installation program allows you to specify the location to install and enter identification information. Here are the steps:

1. If you have any applications running, exit them now.

2. If Windows®95 is already running, then go to Step 3. If Windows is not running, then start Windows.

3. Move the mouse pointer to the Windows®95 Taskbar and click the Start button.

4. From the Windows®95 Start menu, click on **Settings**, then **Control Panel**. In the **Control Panel** dialog box, double-click on the **Add/Remove Programs** icon.

5. The Add/Remove Programs Properties dialog box will appear. Click on the Install button.

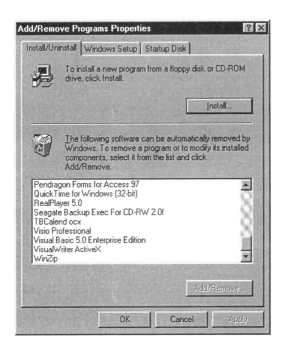

6. The Install Program From Floppy Disk or CD-ROM dialog box will appear. Check to be sure the Installation CD is in the drive, and click on the Next button.

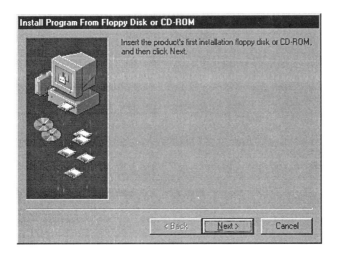

7. The Run Installation Program dialog box will appear. Enter the following command in the command line: E:\SETUP.EXE **NOTE:** E should correspond with the letter designated for your CD-ROM drive. If your CD-ROM drive designation is a letter other than E, please enter that letter instead. Click on the Finish button to proceed with installation.

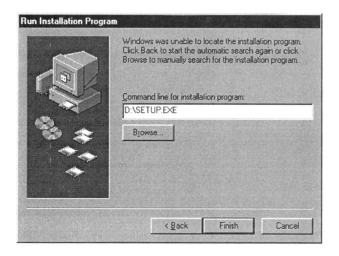

8. The installation background image will appear. Then the Setup Progress indicator will appear. The installation program is preparing for installation. Nothing is required of you at this point.

9. The **Welcome** dialog box will appear stating that all other programs should be exited before running the installation program. Click on the **Next** button to continue.

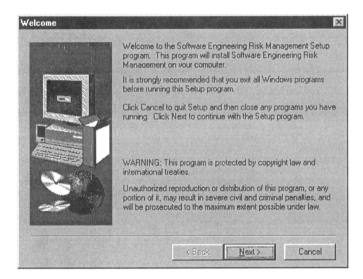

10. The **User Information** dialog box will appear. Enter your name and your company name. Click the **Next** button to continue.

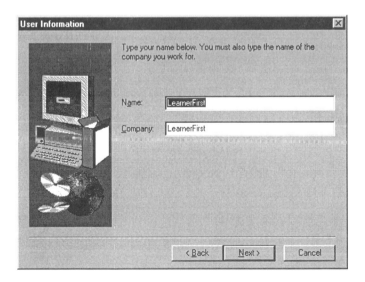

11. The **Choose Destination Location** dialog box will appear, giving you the option of installing the software application in a directory other than the default. However, we recommend using the default installation settings:

C:\Program Files\LearnerFirst\SERIM

Click the **Next** button to continue.

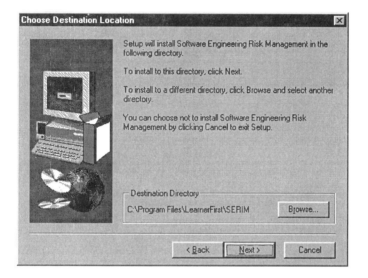

12. The **Select Program Folder** dialog box will appear. If you desire, you can change the default. However, we recommend that you use the default setting (LearnerFirst). Click on the **Next** button to continue with the installation.

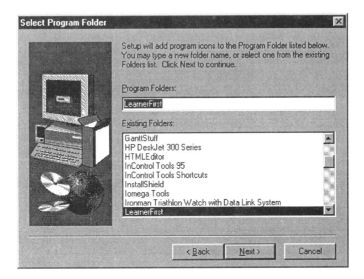

13. The **Start Copying Files** dialog box will appear. Verify that the information in the **Current Settings** box is correct. Click on the **Next** button to continue. Click on the **Back** button to change settings.

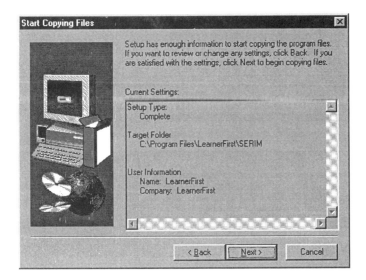

14. The installation program will display a series of dialog boxes indicating the status of the installation. Nothing is required of you at this time.

15. The **Setup Complete** dialog box will appear. We recommend that you restart your computer at this time by clicking on the button beside the statement **Yes, I want to restart my computer now**. Then click on the **Finish** button to complete the installation process.

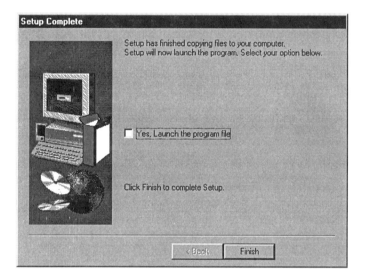

The SERIM application is installed and ready for use! **NOTE:** There are three sample project files that you can use to become better acquainted with the contents and functionality of this application. In this Reference Guide, refer to the section entitled **WORKING WITH SERIM: Examples**.

UNINSTALLING SERIM

To remove the application from your computer, complete the following steps in order. **NOTE**: The images you see on your computer screen may look somewhat different from the pictures included in this manual, due to differences in computer settings and configurations.

1. If you have any applications running, exit them now.

2. If Windows®95 is already running, then go to Step 3. If Windows is not running, then start Windows.

3. Move the mouse pointer to the Windows®95 Taskbar and click the **Start** button.

4. From the Windows®95 Start menu, click on **Settings**, then **Control Panel**. In the **Control Panel** dialog box, double-click on the **Add/Remove Programs** icon.

5. In the Add/Remove Programs Properties dialog box, click on Software Engineering Risk Management. Then click on the Add/Remove button, and finally click on OK.

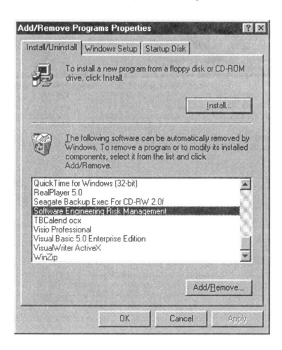

6. The Confirm File Deletion dialog box will appear. Click on Yes.

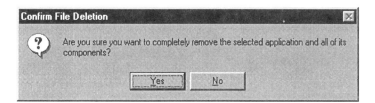

7. The **Remove Shared File?** dialog box may appear. During installation, Borland Database Engine files were installed that may be used by other software applications such as Delphi 3 and Interbase. If you do not use Delphi 3 or Interbase applications, it is safe to remove these files by clicking on **Yes To All**. If the software applications mentioned above are installed on your computer, or you are unsure if they are installed on your computer, click on **No to All**.

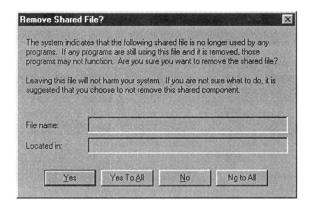

8. If you clicked on **Yes To All** in the previous step, a **Remove Shared File?** confirmation box will appear. Click on **Yes** to remove the shared files. Click on **No** to leave the shared files in place.

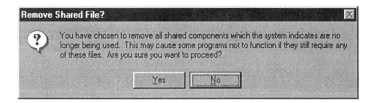

9. A **Remove Programs From Your Computer** dialog box will appear, indicating the status of application removal. SERIM files have been removed from your computer. Click on **OK** to close.

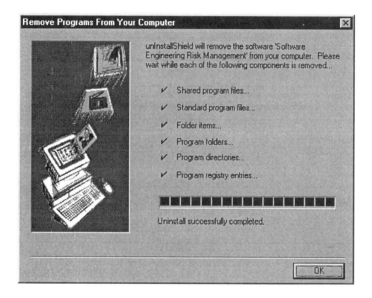

10. The Add/Remove Program Properties dialog box will appear,
    showing that Software Engineering Risk Management has been
    removed from your system. Software Engineering Risk
    Management should no longer appear in the list box. Click on OK
    to close the dialog box.

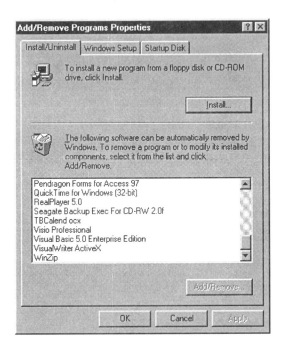

The Software Engineering Risk Management application
(including icons, registry entries, program groups, example projects,
and help file) has now been removed from your computer. NOTE:
All project files created within the SERIM application will remain in
the directory in which they were saved. If you wish to delete all
traces of the application, these files and directories must be deleted
separately.

STARTING SERIM

This section contains basic step-by-step instructions for starting the SERIM software application. **NOTE**: The images you see on your computer screen may look somewhat different from the pictures included in this manual, due to differences in computer settings and configurations.

Instructions
1. Move the mouse pointer to the Windows®95 Taskbar, and click on the **Start** button. This will bring up the **Start** menu.

2. From the **Start** menu, click on **Programs**, then **LearnerFirst**, then **Software Engineering Risk Management**.

3. The **Welcome Screen** will appear. **NOTE:** If you wish to turn off this screen so that it does not appear each time you start the application, click on the check box in the lower left corner of the screen.

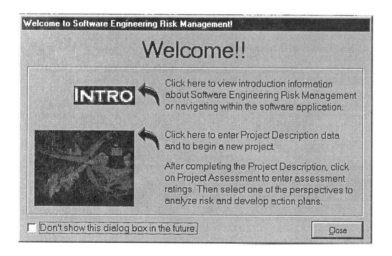

4. Click on INTRO to go directly to introductory information about the application's contents, and navigating within the application. Click on the image of the explorer to go directly to the **Project Description** module, and begin entering descriptive data about your project.

5. After closing the **Welcome Screen**, the next screen to appear will be the **Main Screen**. Click on the **Main Screen** images to navigate to the modules and steps in the application.

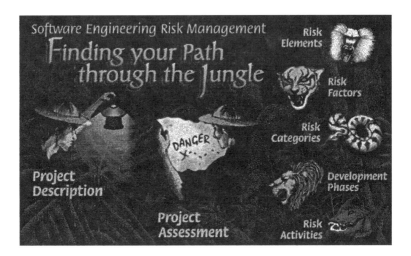

USING SERIM: The Command Structure

The SERIM Command Structure is organized to help you navigate within the application, and accomplish the work of assessing risks for your software development projects. **NOTE:** Navigation is the process used to go to a desired place in the application. As you become more familiar with the SERIM navigation process, you will be able to go quickly to any step in the application and accomplish your objective. If you have used other Windows®95 applications, you will find that this application's windows work the same way. To facilitate your work, these commands are contained within the Top Toolbar, the Main Screen, and the Bottom Toolbar. The functionality of the command structure and the components of the windows are explained in detail within this section.

The Title Bar

The Title Bar is located along the top of a window. It contains the name of the application and the name of the file that is currently open. To move the application window to a different location on your screen, click on the Title Bar, hold the mouse button down, "drag" the title bar to the desired location, and then release the mouse button. **NOTE:** You can also move dialog boxes by dragging their Title Bars.

The Top Toolbar

This toolbar is displayed across the top of the application window. It provides a quick means of navigation with your mouse, as well as access to the many tools used in the application. To select a command from the Top Toolbar, position your cursor over the word for the desired command, and click the left mouse button once. Notice that as you position your cursor over each word, the word is highlighted, and the cursor arrow changes to a pointing finger. These changes indicate that the command you have selected is active in your current window.

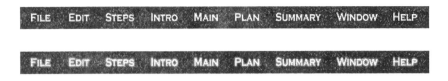

Instructions

1. Click on one of the words (menu or screen commands) in the Top Toolbar. For most commands, a drop-down menu will appear that displays further options for selection.
2. Click on the desired option in the drop-down menu to select that option.

FILE Commands

The FILE drop down menu contains seven options that will allow you to set up and manage your files within the application.

Instructions

1. Click on the word FILE in the Top Toolbar. The FILE drop-down menu will appear.

2. Click on the desired command in the drop-down menu. Specific instructions for each command are described below.

New

Use this command to create a new file. Create a new file each time you begin a new project. **NOTE:** If you have work in progress, you will be asked to save it before creating a new file.

Open

Use this command to open an existing file. The name of all SERIM project files (*.srm) will be listed in the current directory.

Instructions
1. Click on Open. The Open dialog box will appear.

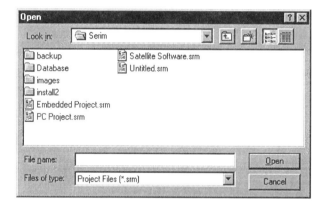

- Click on the arrow to the right of the **Look in:** box to select the drive/directory/folder in which the file is stored.
- Click on the name of the file you wish to open, or type or select the name of the file you wish to open in the **File Name** box.
2. Click the **Open** button to retrieve the file, or the **Cancel** button to exit the dialog box without opening a file.

Save

Use this command when you wish to save the contents of your active file under its current name and location. If you want to change the name or location of an existing file before you save it, use the **Save As** command. **NOTE:** If you are working in untitled.srm, the **Save As** dialog box will appear

Instructions
1. Click on **Save**. The application will now save your most recent changes.
2. If this is the first time you have saved the file, the **Save As** dialog box will appear. You will need to enter your file name.

Save As

Use this command when you wish to change the name or location of an existing file. The dialog box that appears with this command will enable you to name your file and save it to the drive/directory/folder you select.

Instructions
1. Click on **Save As**. The **Save As** dialog box will appear.

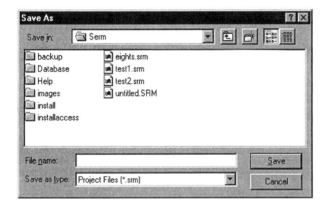

*   Click on the arrow to the right of the **Save in** box to select the drive/directory/folder in which you wish to save your file.
*   Click the cursor inside the **File name** box, and enter the name of your file. **NOTE:** The file name should be a descriptive name of up to eight characters. Choose a file name that relates to the name of your project.
*   Click on the **Save as type** box to select the file format for your file.
2. Click on the **Save** button to save your file with the parameters you have selected. Click on the **Cancel** button to exit the dialog box without saving a file.

Print

Use this command to control how you print reports. To specify a printer and its connection, use the **Print Setup** command.

Instructions

1. Click on **Print**. The Windows®95 **Print** dialog box will appear.

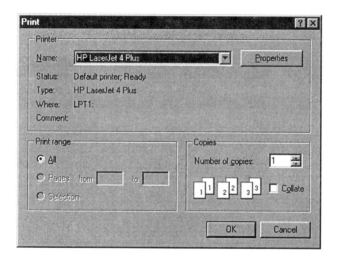

- Click on the up arrow beside **Number of copies** if you need more than one copy of the report.
- Verify that the printer name shown is the correct printer. If you need to change the printer, click the arrow at the end of the **Name** box, and select the correct printer.
- Click on the **Properties** button to verify that **Portrait** is selected.

2. Click the **OK** button to print the selected report. Click on the CANCEL button to exit the dialog box without printing a report.

Print Preview

Activating this command will allow you to view a selected report on screen before you print it.

<u>Instructions</u>
1. Click on Print in the drop-down menu. The Report Print dialog box
   will appear.

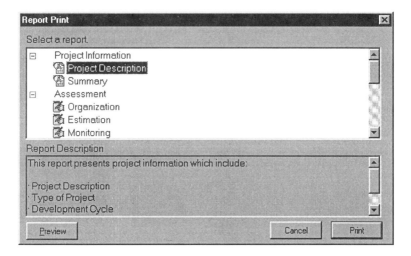

2. Click on the title of the report you wish to print from the list of
   reports in the selection box. The title of the selected report then will
   be highlighted in blue, and a description of the report will appear in
   the Report Description box.
3. Click on the Preview button if you would like to view your report on
   the screen before you print it out. A window will appear, as shown in
   the example below. When your preview is complete, click on the
   Close button to return to the Select a Report dialog box.

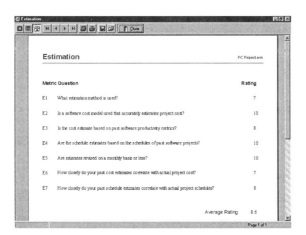

4. Click on the **OK** button in the lower right corner of the **Select a Report** dialog box. The Windows®95 **Print** dialog box will appear.

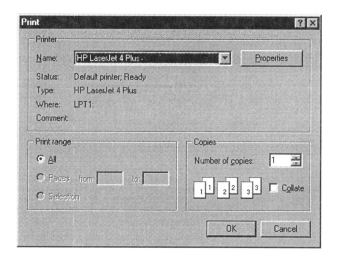

*   Click on the up arrow beside **Number of copies** if you need more than one copy of the report.
*   Verify that the printer name shown is the correct printer. If you need to change the printer, click the arrow at the end of the **Name** box, and select the correct printer.
*   Click on the **Properties** button to verify that **Portrait** is selected.
5. Click the **OK** button to print the selected report. Click on the CANCEL button to exit the dialog box without printing the report.

Exit
Use this command to end your session and exit the SERIM application.

Instructions
1. Click on **Exit** in the drop-down menu. If you have made changes to your file since you last saved, the application will ask if you want to save them.
2. Click **Yes** if you want to save changes, or click **No** if you do not want to save changes. If you decide not to exit the application at this point, then click **Cancel**.

Edit Commands

In this application, you can move information from one place to another. The Edit commands can save a great deal of time by helping you to avoid re-typing information.

Instructions
1. Click on the word Edit in the Top Toolbar. The Edit drop-down menu will appear.

2. Click on the desired command in the drop-down menu. Specific instructions for each command are described below.

Cut
This command removes selected (highlighted) information from an edit box and puts it on the Windows®95 Clipboard. The Clipboard can only hold one block of information at a time, so cutting information to the clipboard replaces any contents previously stored there. **NOTE:** The Cut command is only available if you have selected (highlighted) information.

Instructions
1. Select (Highlight) the information that you wish to cut.
2. Click on Edit in the Top Toolbar. The Edit drop-down menu will appear.
3. Click on Cut. The highlighted information will be cut from the existing text, and placed on the clipboard.

Copy
Use this command to copy selected (highlighted) information onto the Windows®95 Clipboard. Copying information to the Clipboard replaces any contents previously stored there. When you copy information to the clipboard, the selected information will also remain in its original

location. **NOTE:** This command is only available if you have selected (highlighted) information.

Instructions
1. Select (Highlight) the information that you wish to copy.
2. Click on EDIT in the Top Toolbar. The EDIT drop-down menu will appear.
3. Click on Copy. A copy of the highlighted information will be placed on the clipboard.

Paste

This command pastes (inserts) a copy of the Clipboard contents at the cursor's position. **NOTE: Paste** is only available if the Clipboard contains information that you have cut or copied to it.

Instructions
1. Place the cursor where you would like to paste (insert) the information from the clipboard.
2. Click on EDIT in the Top Toolbar. The EDIT drop-down menu will appear.
3. Click on Paste. The clipboard information will be inserted at the location of your cursor.

STEPS Command

The STEPS command provides a way for you to go quickly and directly to any module or step in the application.

1. Click on the word STEPS in the Top Toolbar. The STEPS drop-down menu will appear.

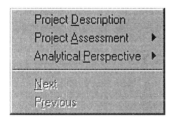

2. Click on the desired command in the drop-down menu. Specific
    instructions for each command are described below.

Project Description

Click on Project Description to go directly to the Project Description
Module, and begin entering descriptive data about your project.

Project Assessment

Click on Project Assessment to begin assigning ratings to the metric
questions for any of the ten major categories of software risk factors.

*   Organization
*   Estimation
*   Monitoring
*   Development Methodology
*   Tools
*   Risk Culture
*   Usability
*   Correctness
*   Reliability
*   Personnel

Instructions

1. Click on Project Assessment. The following drop-down menu will
    appear.

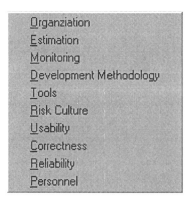

2. Click on the name of any assessment risk factor category to go directly to that step in the application.

Analytical Perspectives

Click on Analytical Perspectives to go directly to any of the five perspectives, and analyze your project's assessment scores.

- Risk Factors
- Risk Elements
- Risk Categories
- Risk Activities
- Development Phases

Instructions

1. Click on Analytical Perspective. The following drop-down menu will appear.

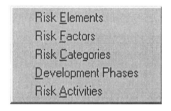

Risk Elements
Risk Factors
Risk Categories
Development Phases
Risk Activities

2. Click on the name of any analytical perspective to go directly to that step in the application.

Next

As you work within the application, the Next command will take you directly from your current step to the next step in the application.

Previous

As you work within the application, the Previous command will take you directly from your current step to the preceding step in the application.

INTRO Command

This command allows you to go directly to the introduction to the SERIM Application. When you click on INTRO, the following drop-down menu will appear.

1. Click on **Navigation** to see information about navigating within the application.
2. Click on **Software Engineering Risk Management** to see information about the contents of the application.
3. Click on **Show Welcome at Startup** to turn the Welcome Screen on and off. **NOTE:** When you see the check mark ✓, the Welcome Screen will appear each time you start the application.

MAIN Command

This command will take you directly to the **Main Screen** of the application. The **Main Screen** for SERIM is designed to help you navigate between the major modules and steps of the application. Use the **Main Screen** to go quickly to a particular module. **NOTE:** If the **Main Screen** is already open, this command will not be active.

PLAN Command

This command will allow you to go directly to the form for creating an action plan.

Instructions – To Create your First Action Plan
1. Click on PLAN in the Top Toolbar. The following window will appear.

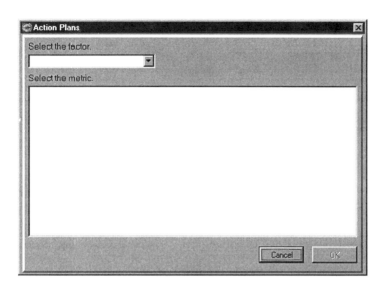

2. Click on the desired risk factor from the list in the top box. Then click on the desired metric question in the bottom box.

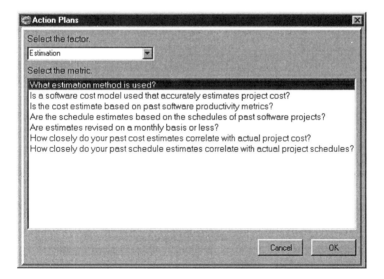

3. Click on OK to bring up the Action Plans data entry screen. Click on Cancel to close this screen and return to the Main Screen. NOTE: You will notice that the risk factor you selected, the Metric ID, and the rating you assigned to this metric question appear at the top of the screen.

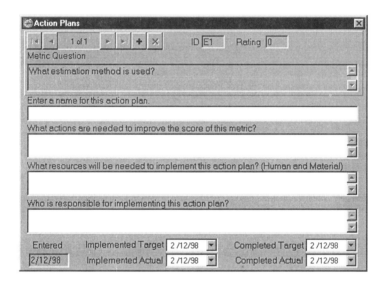

4. Enter the appropriate information in the four data entry boxes. NOTE: The Entered box contains the date the action plan was created. This box is "read only."
5. Enter dates for Implemented Target and Implemented Actual.
6. Click on the **x** in the top right corner of the screen to return to the Main Screen.

Instructions – To Create Additional Action Plans
1. Click on PLAN in the Top Toolbar. The Action Plans screen will appear.

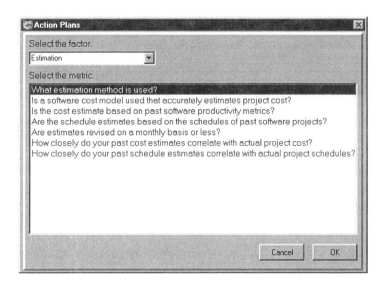

2. Click on the desired risk factor from the list in the top box. Then click on the desired metric question in the bottom box.

3. Click on **OK** to bring up the **Action Plans** data entry screen. Click on **Cancel** to close this screen and return to the **Main Screen**.

4. Click on the + sign in the data control box located at the top left of the screen. The following window will appear. **NOTE:** You will notice that the Metric Question you selected, the Metric ID, and the rating you assigned to this question appear at the top of the screen.

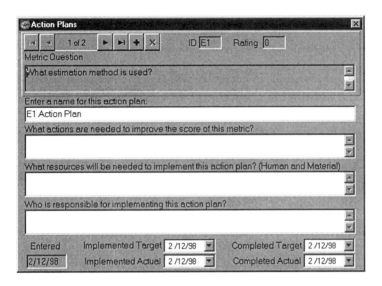

5. Enter the appropriate information in the four data entry boxes.
    NOTE: The Entered box contains the date the action plan was
    created. This box is "read only."
6. Enter dates for Implemented Target and Implemented Actual.
7. Click on the **x** in the top right corner of the screen to return to the
    Main Screen.

Instructions – To Modify Existing Action Plans
1. Click on Plan in the Top Toolbar. The Action Plans screen will
    appear.

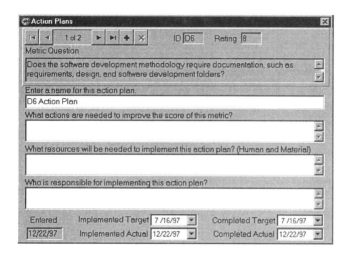

2. Click on the Previous and Next arrows in the data control box to locate your desired Action Plan.
3. Make any needed modifications.
4. Click on the **x** in the top right corner of the screen to return to the Main Screen.

SUMMARY Command

To get a summary of scores for Overall Project, Risk Elements, and Development Phases, click on the word SUMMARY in the Top ToolBar. You will see the summary scores for the project in your current file, as shown in this example.

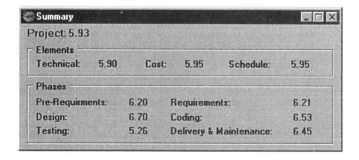

WINDOW Command

The WINDOW command allows you to overlay and position your open windows in three different ways.

1. Click on the word WINDOW in the Top Toolbar. The WINDOW drop-down menu will appear.

2. Click on the desired command in the drop-down menu. Specific instructions for each command are described below.

Tile
Click on Tile to make all your open windows the same size. Each new window you open will be visible on the screen, and will appear the same size as the other windows.

Cascade
Click on Cascade to arrange all open windows so that they overlap. You will be able to see the corners of any windows that underlie the top window.

Arrange All
Click on Arrange All to arrange the minimized title bars of your windows so they are evenly spaced on the screen, and don't overlap. **NOTE:** You must minimize each window first, as the minimized title bars of all windows will be visible on the screen at the same time.

HELP Command

You can access help within the SERIM application by clicking on the word HELP in the Top Toolbar. **NOTE:** You can also access help by pressing the F1 key, or clicking on the green question mark icon wherever it appears.

Instructions
1. Click on the word HELP in the Top Toolbar. The HELP drop-down menu will appear.

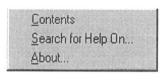

2. Click on the desired command in the drop-down menu. Specific instructions for each command are described below.

Contents

Opens the Help Topics dialog box with the Contents tab selected, displaying a hierarchical list of the help topics.

Instructions
1. Click on the word HELP in the Top Toolbar. The HELP dialog box will appear.
2. Click on the tab at the top of the dialog box that displays the list of help topics in the manner you desire.
    *   Click on the Contents tab to see a hierarchical list of HELP topics. **NOTE:** This tab will be open when the dialog box first appears.
    *   Click on the Find tab to conduct a full-text search of HELP.
3. Click on your desired topic. The help information related to that topic will appear.

Search for Help On

Opens the Help Topics dialog box with the Index tab selected.

Instructions
1. Click on the word HELP in the Top Toolbar. The HELP dialog box will appear.
2. Click on the Index tab to see an alphabetical list of help topics.
3. Click on your desired topic. The help information related to that topic will appear.

About

Shows copyright and version information for the Software Engineering
Risk Management application.

The Main Screen

To go to the **Main Screen**, click on the word MAIN in the Top Toolbar.
Once you see the **Main Screen**, you can click on its images to navigate
directly to any of the modules in the application. As you use the **Main
Screen** images for navigation, notice that positioning your cursor over an
image will cause the image to highlight, and the arrow to change to a
pointing finger. You will also see "balloon help" messages that will help
you decide how to proceed within the application.

Instructions
1. Click on the explorer with the lantern to go to the **Project
   Description Module**.
2. Click on the explorer with the map to go to the **Project Assessment
   Module**.
3. Click on the animal that corresponds with the desired perspective to
   go to one of the five **Analytical Perspectives**.

The Bottom Toolbar

At the bottom of each window in a series of screens, the Bottom Toolbar
will appear. The purpose of the Bottom Toolbar is to:
• Allow you to navigate to the next or previous screens.
• Close, Save, or Cancel the work you have completed in the screens.

Instructions

1. Click on the row of paw prints on the right end of the Bottom Toolbar to navigate to the next screen in a series.

2. Click on the row of paw prints on the left end of the Bottom Toolbar to navigate to the previous screen in a series.

3. Click on the word **Close** to close the current screen (and window) and save your work.

4. Click the on the word **Save** to save your work and remain in the current screen.

5. Click on the word **Cancel** to close the current screen (and window) without saving any changes.

Scroll Bars

When a screen image is larger than the size of a window, use the Scroll Bar to move the image, so you can see the parts that are not currently visible. Vertical Scroll Bars are displayed at the right edge of windows or data entry fields, as shown below. Horizontal Scroll Bars are displayed at the bottom of windows or data entry fields. Both types of Scroll Bars work in a similar manner.

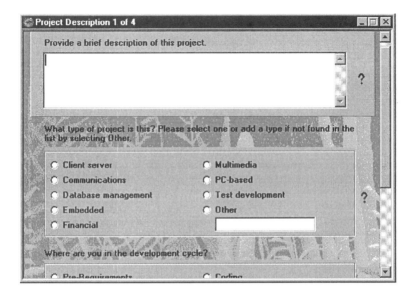

Instructions - Vertical Scroll Bar
1. Click on the arrow pointing up to move the screen image down.
2. Click on the arrow pointing down to move the screen image up.
3. Click on the movable, rectangular, portion of the Scroll Bar (if the Scroll Bar contains this component) and hold the mouse button down. Slide the cursor up or down, until the screen image is positioned within the window, as you desire. Then release the mouse button, position the cursor on the screen, and click once more to fix the screen image in its current position.

Instructions - Horizontal Scroll Bar
1. Click on the arrow on the right end of the bar to move the screen image to the left.
2. Click on the arrow on the left end of the bar to move the screen image to the right.
3. Click on the movable, rectangular, portion of the Scroll Bar (if the Scroll Bar contains this component) and hold the mouse button down. Slide the cursor right or left, until the screen image is positioned within the window, as you desire. Then release the mouse button, position the cursor on the screen, and click once more to fix the screen in its current position.

EXPLORING SERIM: Application Contents

Project Description

To enter this section from the **Main Screen**, click on the explorer with the lantern, or select STEPS, **Project Description** from the Top Toolbar.

In this section, you will be prompted to enter some basic information to identify your project. The data entry fields include:
- A brief description of the project
- Type of project
- Where you are in the development cycle
- Project Start Date
- Projected Completion Date

When you have completed your data entry for Project Description, please return to the main screen by clicking on CLOSE at the bottom of the screen. (You may also return to the main screen by clicking on CANCEL, but the data entered will not be saved.)

Project Assessment

To enter this section from the **Main Screen**, click on the explorer with the map, or select STEPS, **Project Assessment** from the Top Toolbar.

The goal of the SERIM application is to help you find a safer path through the software development jungle by assessing the major risk factors that are waiting to devour your projects. Each risk factor contains a series of metric questions you will rate on a scale of 0 to 10. **NOTE:** If a question does not apply to your project, assign a rating of "*", for "not applicable". Your ratings will then be used in the SERIM formulas to predict project risk. The major factors influencing risk in software development include:

- **Organization**
- **Estimation**
- **Monitoring**
- **Development Methodology**
- **Tools**
- **Risk Culture**
- **Usability**
- **Correctness**
- **Reliability**
- **Personnel**

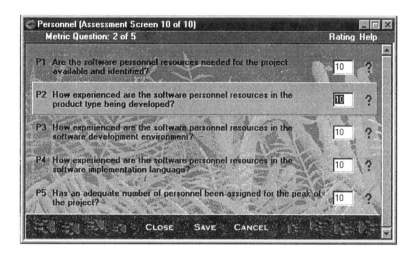

This is the image of one of the assessment data entry screens. At the top of the assessment screens, the blue title bar tells you where you are in the list of the ten assessment risk factors. The green information bar tells you the number of your current question out of the total number of questions within the current risk factor. As you look down the screen, you will see that each metric question is labeled with a metric ID letter and number. To rate a metric question, enter a number between 0 and 10 in the data entry box beside the question. **NOTE:** If the question is not applicable to your project, enter an asterisk * in the data entry box. Then use the Tab key to move the cursor to the next data entry box. As you Tab to each successive question, you will notice that a gray perspective box moves the current question into the foreground. If you need help or further information before entering a rating for any metric question, click on the green question mark beside that question, or press the F1 key.

When you have completed your SERIM assessment, please return to the Main Screen by clicking CLOSE in the Bottom Toolbar. You may also return to the Main Screen by clicking CANCEL, but your data will not be saved. **NOTE:** The use of the Bottom Toolbar was explained in detail in the previous section of this Reference Guide. When you have returned to the Main Screen, continue in the application by choosing one of the five Analytical Perspectives to begin analyzing your project's risk data. To choose a perspective, click on the animal representing the desired perspective.

Analytical Perspectives

To select an Analytical Perspective from the Main Screen, click on the animal representing your desired perspective, or select STEPS, Analytical Perspective from the Top Toolbar. You can then analyze your project's risks from any or all of the following five perspectives.

- **Risk Factors**
- **Risk Elements**
- **Risk Categories**
- **Risk Activities**
- **Development Phases**

Once you have completed the assessment module, the application will calculate your project's risk scores. When you select an Analytical Perspective, these scores will be displayed in a series of bar graphs. You can then "drill down" within each perspective to the scores of the individual Metric Questions, so that you can create Action Plans to improve these scores.

To illustrate the "drill down" process within an Analytical Perspective, let's work through an example. In this example, Development Phases was the perspective selected. Notice that the name of our selection appears in black print above the bar graph, on the left. The score for each Development Phase is displayed on the bar graph, and the overall Project Risk score is displayed in blue print above the bar graph, on the right. **NOTE:** To obtain help related to any item in the list box at the top of the screen, single-click on the desired item, and then click on the green question mark to the right of the list box, or press F1. To obtain additional information about information displayed in the bar graph, single-click on the green question mark to the left of the bar graph, or press F1. To go to the next screen, select an item in the list box and click on the right paw prints, or double click an item in the list box.

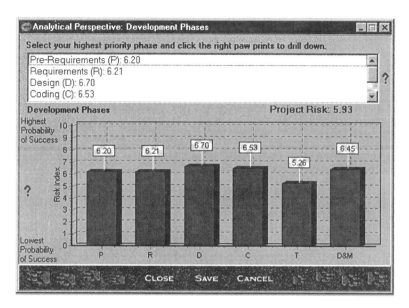

In the next example, we have "drilled down" within the Development Phases perspective by double-clicking on the Coding phase in the list box at the top of the screen. Notice that "Coding" now appears after "Development Phases" in black print above the bar graph, to indicate our selection.

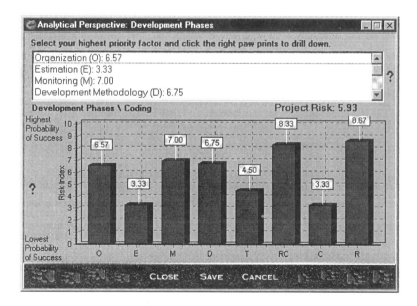

Next, we have "drilled down" within the Coding phase by double-clicking on the Risk Factor in the list box at the top of the screen. Notice that the name of the Risk Factor we selected (Organization) has now been added to Development Phases\Coding\ above the bar graph.

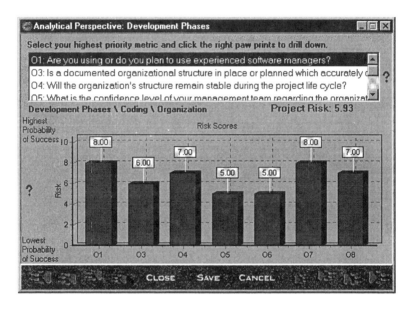

Finally, we have "drilled down" within the Organization Risk Factor by double-clicking on the Metric Question in the list box at the top of the screen. Notice that the Metric Question ID (O3), the rating you assigned to this Metric Question (5), and the Metric Question itself appear at the top of the screen. You can begin creating your action plan for this metric question by entering information in the data entry boxes. **NOTE:** Once an action plan has been created for a metric question, you will notice that the letters for that question turn bright blue in the list box on the previous screen. This is to remind you that you have already completed an action plan for all the questions displayed in bright blue print.

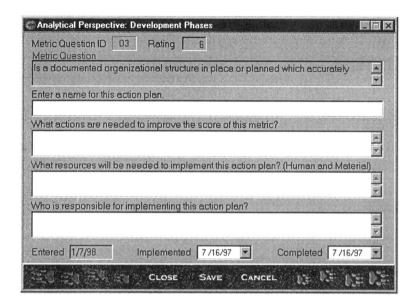

When you have completed your risk analysis from any of the perspectives, please return to the Main Screen, by clicking on CLOSE at the bottom of the screen. You may also return to the Main Screen by clicking on CANCEL, but the data you entered will not be saved. **NOTE**: The options CLOSE and SAVE are only active on the action plan entry screen. You can then choose another Analytical Perspective if you wish, by clicking on the animal representing the desired perspective. You may work through any or all of the Analytical Perspectives, in any order you choose.

Risk Factors

This perspective helps you to analyze how each of the ten risk factors impacts your project in the following areas.

- **Organization** - Assesses risks associated with the maturity of the organization's structure, communications, functions, and leadership.
- **Estimation** - Assesses risks associated with inaccurate estimations of the resources, schedules, and costs needed to develop software.
- **Monitoring** - Assesses risks associated with planning, tracking, and reporting for a software development project.
- **Development Methodology** - Assesses risks associated with potential problems in selection and use of the methodology for a software development project.
- **Tools** - Assesses risks associated with the selection, use, and degree of automation of the tools used for software development.
- **Risk Culture** - Assesses the risks associated with risk management practices and management decision-making processes related to trade-offs in risk vs. profit.
- **Usability** - Assesses risks associated with the documentation and functionality of the software product once it is delivered to the end user.
- **Correctness** - Assesses risks associated with identification, documentation, and tracing of customer requirements, and the resolution of action items prior to delivery.
- **Reliability** - Assesses risks associated with error handling, faults, defects, and testing.
- **Personnel** - Assesses risks associated with the number, availability, knowledge and experience of the software personnel assigned to the project.

Certain factors and characteristics are associated with software development risk. Rowe [1] places risk factors for risk valuation and evaluation into the following categories.
- Type of consequence: voluntary/involuntary, immediate/delayed, statistical/identifiable, controlled/uncontrolled.
- Nature of consequence: cultural values, magnitude of consequences, origination of risk event, degree of knowledge,
- Other factors: magnitude of probability, situational factors, psychological behavior of groups and individuals.

Although not directly related to software, the idea of identifying risk factors has merit. Identifying factors describing software characteristics have been used in the past. Research by McCall et al. [2] and Boehm et al. [3] has identified factors related to software quality and reliability.

Shumskas [4] and Cooper [5] identified software risk factors from a software procurement perspective. Just-in-Time (JIT) software uses factors to reflect general risk associated with the development of software.

These factors encapsulate risks associated with software. Software risk factors identify relationships between the risk elements previously identified in terms of items more closely related to software issues.

As shown in the following table, a risk factor can relate to more than one risk element. Risk perspectives and risk activities have similar relationships since a risk activity can relate to more than one risk perspective. This table identifies the influence of each software risk factor on each of the risk elements. Based on industry experience, each risk factor has been given a value of high, medium, or low, identifying its degree of influence on the software risk elements.

Influence of Software Risk Factors on Risk Elements

SOFTWARE RISK FACTOR	SOFTWARE RISK ELEMENT		
	Technical	Cost	Schedule
Organization	Low	High	High
Estimation	Low	High	High
Monitoring	Medium	High	High
Development Methodology	Medium	High	High
Tools	Medium	Medium	Medium
Risk Culture	High	Medium	Medium
Usability	High	Low	Low
Correctness	High	Low	Low
Reliability	High	Low	Low
Personnel	High	High	High

Another way to view software risk factors is to examine their relationship to the software development process or the software product. This influence is identified as either **major** or **minor** (see the table below). Based on industry experience, the terms **major** and **minor** reflect the degree of influence that these factors have on the software development process or product.

Software Risk Factors' Influence Against the
Software Categories Process and Product

SOFTWARE RISK FACTOR	SOFTWARE RISK CATEGORY	
	Process	Product
Organization	Major	Minor
Estimation	Major	Minor
Monitoring	Major	Minor
Development Methodology	Major	Minor
Tools	Major	Major
Risk Culture	Major	Major
Usability	Minor	Major
Correctness	Minor	Major
Reliability	Minor	Major
Personnel	Major	Major

Choices exist when making decisions concerning risks on software projects. The model presented here has been based on the three-step process of problem solving using models to help evaluate risks (this is defined by Holloway [6]). The first step is to analyze alternatives. Alternatives exist when deciding activities based on risks. The second step is to create a model that will evaluate alternatives. The model should help in the decision-making process by assessing the alternatives. The third step is to make a choice. If a choice is not made, the passing of time will dictate the choices for you.

The Software Engineering Risk Model (SERIM) used in JIT software is based on the premise that software development management alternatives are always present. As such, the model uses the form of a probability tree [7] addressing decision alternatives and the use of probabilities.

Organization

The software risk factor ORGANIZATION addresses risks associated with the maturity of the organization's structure, communications, functions, and leadership. Since the organization's efficiency and maturity has a major influence on how smoothly the project is completed, this factor has a high influence on the software risk elements of cost and schedule. However, since it does not address how and what will be implemented in software or its results, the risk factor ORGANIZATION has a low influence on the technical software product. This factor is also a major influence on the process of developing software, since it will affect the efficiency of the human and computer resources that will be available to develop the software. Conversely, ORGANIZATION is a minor influence on the product, since the software developers have more direct control over the implementation of the software.

Purpose
The purpose of this step is to present eight questions related to the software risk factor ORGANIZATION. By rating each of these questions on a scale of 0 to 10 (enter a rating of "*" if the question does not apply to your project), you will generate the SERIM metrics to measure your project's potential risks related to this factor. You can then develop action plans to raise the score of any metric question.

Metric questions
O1   Are you using, or do you plan to use, experienced software managers?

O2   Has your company produced software similar to this in the past?

O3   Is a documented organizational structure in place or planned which accurately describes communication channels and lines of authority?

O4   Will the organization's structure remain stable during the project life cycle?

O5   What is the confidence level of your management team regarding the organization's ability to deliver the software product on time, on or below budget, and with high quality?

O6   Do good communications exist between the different organizations supporting the development of the software project?

O7   Are software configuration management functions being performed?

O8   Are software quality functions being performed?

Estimation

The software risk factor ESTIMATION focuses on risks associated with inaccurate estimations of the resources, schedules, and costs needed to develop software. This factor has a high influence on the software risk elements of cost and schedule, since inaccurate or missing estimation techniques and models for software address these issues. However, it has a low influence on the technical software product, since it does not influence how and what will be implemented in software or its results. ESTIMATION is considered to be of major importance to the process of developing software, since it will influence the amount of human and computer resources that will be available to develop the software. As previously mentioned, it has a minor influence on the product.

Purpose
The purpose of this step is to present seven questions related to the software risk factor ESTIMATION. By rating each of these questions on a scale of 0 to 10 (enter a rating of "*" if the question does not apply to your project), you will generate the SERIM metrics to measure your project's potential risks related to this factor. You can then develop action plans to raise the score of any metric question.

Metric questions
E1   What estimation method is used?
E2   Is a software cost model used that accurately estimates project cost?
E3   Is the cost estimate based on past software productivity metrics?
E4   Are the schedule estimates based on the schedules of past software projects?
E5   Are estimates revised on a monthly basis or less?
E6   How closely do your past cost estimates correlate with actual project cost?
E7   How closely do your past schedule estimates correlate with actual project schedules?

Monitoring

The software risk factor MONITORING refers to risks associated with identifying problems. Since most monitoring techniques relate to cost and schedule, this factor has a high influence on risks associated with meeting milestones and budgets. Since most monitoring techniques on software implementation only give a partial picture of what to expect of the product prior to delivery, they only have a medium influence on the software technical product. Software risk factor MONITORING has a major influence on the software development process since the results of the monitoring may influence how the software is completed. Because most software monitoring techniques do not influence the technical implementation of the software solution, it has only a minor influence on the product.

Purpose
The purpose of this step is to present seven questions related to the software risk factor MONITORING. By rating each of these questions on a scale of 0 to 10 (enter a rating of "*" if the question does not apply to your project), you will generate the SERIM metrics to measure your project's potential risks related to this factor. You can then develop action plans to raise the score of any metric question.

Metric questions
M1 Are distinct milestones set for every development phase of each major software project?

M2 Is a detailed WBS used to track and report costs and budget for each piece of major software development?

M3 Is there a monitoring system setup to track cost, schedule, and earned-value?

M4 Are cost, schedule, and earned-value reports available on demand?

M5 Are cost, schedule and earned-value reports updated on a monthly basis, or more frequently?

M6 Is there a problem or action log system that is used and updated on a weekly basis?

M7 Is there a process for addressing and recording technical problems that is used and updated weekly?

Development Methodology

Software risk factor DEVELOPMENT METHODOLOGY identifies the methods by which software is developed. This risk factor has a medium impact on the technical element, and high impact on the cost and schedule elements for the following reasons. The development methodology approach will only have limited influence on the technical solution implemented in software through its architecture, design assumptions, and so forth. Depending on the time it takes to implement the development approach of the software or the additional cost savings the methodology may have, this factor highly influences the costs and schedule. DEVELOPMENT METHODOLOGY rates as a major influence on the software process since it determines the steps involved in producing software. It has a minor influence on the technical product since many different development methodologies can produce software that will satisfy the end user.

Purpose
The purpose of this step is to present seven questions related to the software risk factor DEVELOPMENT METHODOLOGY. By rating each of these questions on a scale of 0 to 10 (enter a rating of "*" if the question does not apply to your project), you will generate the SERIM metrics to measure your project's potential risks related to this factor. You can then develop action plans to raise the score of any metric question.

Metric questions
D1 Is there a documented software development methodology/plan for the project that is closely followed?

D2 Are the software developers trained in the software development methodology?

D3 How closely is the software development methodology followed?

D4 Does the software development methodology include requirements, design, and code reviews/walkthroughs/inspections?

D5 Does the development methodology require test plans and/or test procedures for all software functions?

D6 Does the software development methodology require documentation, such as requirements, design, and software development folders?

D7 Is software regression testing performed?

Tools

The software risk factor TOOLS focuses on risks associated with the software tools used when software is developed. This risk factor has a medium influence on the technical, cost, and schedule software risk elements for the following reasons. The choice and use of software tools will influence the technical solution implemented in software by its assumptions and by the rules it will enforce and ingrain into the software, but it will not affect meeting the technical requirements. It will also have some influence on the costs and schedule depending on the efficiency, effectiveness, and use of the tool, but it will not have as much influence on how the software solution is estimated or staffed. Software TOOLS have a major influence on the software process since it can shorten or lengthen the process. It also has a major influence on the technical product since tools can automatically check for certain types of design, language constructs, test errors, and so forth, thus making the software a higher-quality product.

Purpose
The purpose of this step is to present nine questions related to the software risk factor TOOLS. By rating each of these questions on a scale of 0 to 10 (enter a rating of "*" if the question does not apply to your project), you will generate the SERIM metrics to measure your project's potential risks related to this factor. You can then develop action plans to raise the score of any metric question.

Metric questions
T1 Are the software developers trained to use the software tools identified for the project?

T2 Are automated tools used for software design?

T3 Are automated tools used for software testing?

T4 Are automated tools used for software test procedure generation?

T5 Are automated tools used for software regression testing?

T6 Are automated tools used for software requirements traceability?

T7 Are automated tools used for software re-engineering (identifying existing characteristics of the software based on its code, such as its structure, data dictionary, etc.)?

T8 How stable is your compiler/linker/debugger?

T9 Are the software tools required for the project readily available to the software developers when needed?

Risk Culture

The management decision-making process in which risks are considered is the software risk factor RISK CULTURE. This risk factor has a high influence on the technical product, since it may cause one to take a less than optimal approach to the software solution, or even to try unproven methods. The decision-making process has a medium impact on cost and schedule elements. This is because staffing and budgets vary, causing slight amounts of underestimation or late staffing. It has a major influence on the software development process, and can have an extreme range, spanning from the use of a more conservative, tired development approach, to attempting a new development approach for the first time. RISK CULTURE also has a major influence on the product, since risks associated with new technology, lack of testing, and other features directly affect the quality of the software or its operation.

Purpose
The purpose of this step is to present eleven questions related to the software risk factor RISK CULTURE. By rating each of these questions on a scale of 0 to 10 (enter a rating of "*" if the question does not apply to your project), you will generate the SERIM metrics to measure your project's potential risks related to this factor. You can then develop action plans to raise the score of any metric question.

Metric questions
RC1 Is your company willing to trade increased budget risks for higher profit?

RC2 Is your company willing to trade increased schedule risks for higher profit?

RC3 Is your company willing to trade increased technical risks for higher profit?

RC4 Is your company willing to trade decreased budget risks for lower profit?

RC5 Is your company willing to trade decreased schedule risk for lower profit?

RC6 Is your company willing to trade decreased technical functionality for lower profit?

RC7 Is your company market-driven?

RC8 Is your company's culture conservative in its decision making?

RC9 How would you rate your company's investment in new products and technology?

RC10 Does your company build new products and/or technology in-house, or acquire them?

RC11 Does your company practice and document formalized risk management procedures?

Usability

Risks associated with the software product once it is delivered to the end user are considered in the software risk factor USABILITY. This risk factor highly influences the technical product, since it may cause inconvenience or delays that will result in additional training for the user. However, this will not affect the overall technical objectives. Since it is related to the delivered software product and usually not measured or tracked as a milestone by itself, USABILITY has a low influence on the cost and schedule risk elements. Thus, software USABILITY has a minor influence on the software development process, but has a major influence on the software product.

Purpose
The purpose of this step is to present six questions related to the software risk factor USABILITY. By rating each of these questions on a scale of 0 to 10 (enter a rating of "*" if the question does not apply to your project), you will generate the SERIM metrics to measure your project's potential risks related to this factor. You can then develop action plans to raise the score of any metric question.

Metric questions

U1   Has the user manual for the software product been developed, tested, and revised?

U2   Are help functions available for each input or output screen?

U3   Is the user involved in reviewing prototype or early versions of the software?

U4   Is the user interface designed to an industry standard or to a standard familiar to the user?

U5   Have user response times been identified?

U6   Has the design been evaluated to minimize keystrokes and data entry?

Correctness

The software risk factor CORRECTNESS deals with risks associated with the software product once it is delivered to the end user. Since it relates to the requirements the customer has defined, this risk factor highly influences the technical product. It has a low influence on the cost and schedule risk elements since it is related to the delivered software product and usually not measured or tracked as a milestone by itself. Because of this, software CORRECTNESS has a minor influence on the software development process but has a major influence on the software product.

Purpose

The purpose of this step is to present nine questions related to the software risk factor CORRECTNESS. By rating each of these questions on a scale of 0 to 10 (enter a rating of "*" if the question does not apply to your project), you will generate the SERIM metrics to measure your project's potential risks related to this factor. You can then develop action plans to raise the score of any metric question.

Metric questions

C1   Have all the software requirements been identified and documented?

C2   Have software requirements been traced to the design?

C3   Have the software requirements been traced to the code?

C4   Have the software requirements been traced to the test procedures?

C5 Have there been, or do you anticipate, many changes to the software requirements?

C6 Are the software designs traceable to the code?

C7 Is the software design traceable to the test procedures?

C8 Have all the open action items been addressed and resolved prior to delivery to the customer?

C9 Has software functional testing been performed prior to customer delivery?

Reliability

The software risk factor RELIABILITY addresses risks associated with the software product once it is delivered to the end user. This risk factor has a high influence on the technical product, because it relates to the error-free execution of the software, which is based on the software correctness. It has a low influence on the cost and schedule risk elements, since it is related to the delivered software product, and usually is not measured or tracked as a milestone by itself. Thus, software RELIABILITY has a minor influence on the software development process, but has a major influence on the software product.

Purpose
The purpose of this step is to present twelve questions related to the software risk factor RELIABILITY. By rating each of these questions on a scale of 0 to 10 (enter a rating of "*" if the question does not apply to your project), you will generate the SERIM metrics to measure your project's potential risks related to this factor. You can then develop action plans to raise the score of any metric questions.

Metric questions
R1 Do error-handling conditions exist for every possible instance within the software design and code?

R2 When an error condition is detected, does processing continue?

R3 Are error tolerances defined for input and output data?

R4 Are inputs checked for valid values before processing begins?

R5 Are hardware faults detected and processed in the software?

R6 Is the use of global data types in the software minimized?

R7 Is defect data collected during software integration?

R8   Is defect data being logged-in and closed-out prior to delivery to the customer?

R9   Is a software reliability model used to predict reliability?

R10 Are test plans used to perform software tests?

R11 Has stress testing been performed?

R12 Does a group separate from the software development group perform software testing?

Personnel

Risks associated with the ability to use the software development methods and tools, and the knowledge to develop software are associated with the software risk factor PERSONNEL. This factor has a high influence on the software risk elements of cost and schedule, since the personnel capabilities assigned to the project have the largest influence on the productivity and the ability to meet milestones (this has been documented by the research of Boehm [8] and Brooks [9]). Since the reasoning skills of the software engineering personnel directly relate to how and what will be implemented in software and the results, PERSONNEL has a high influence on the technical software product. PERSONNEL is also considered to have a major importance regarding the process of developing software, since how the development process is implemented is ultimately determined by the personnel. This factor also has a major importance on the product.

Purpose
The purpose of this step is to present five questions related to the software risk factor PERSONNEL. By rating each of these questions on a scale of 0 to 10 (enter a rating of "*" if the question does not apply to your project), you will generate the SERIM metrics to measure your project's potential risks related to this factor. You can then develop action plans to raise the score of any metric question.

Metric questions
P1   Are the software personnel resources needed for the project available and identified?

P2   How experienced are the software personnel resources in the product type being developed?

P3 How experienced are the software personnel resources in the software development environment?

P4 How experienced are the software personnel resources in the software implementation language?

P5 How many software development personnel will be needed at the peak of the development process?

Risk Elements

This perspective helps you analyze the data from your assessment of the ten Risk Factors as they impact the following Risk Elements.

- **Technical Risks** - Risks associated with the software product, including Functionality, Quality, Reliability, Usability, Timeliness, Maintainability, and Reusability.

- **Cost Risks** - Risks associated with the cost of the software product during software development, including Budget, Nonrecurring Costs, Recurring Costs, Fixed Costs, Variable Costs, Profit/Loss Margin, and Realism.

- **Schedule Risks** - Risks associated with the schedule of the software product during development, including Flexibility, Meeting Established Milestones, and Realism.

Just-In-Time (JIT) takes into account risks from both a technological and a business (financial) perspective [10]. Technical risks include algorithms, technology availability, and the maturity of the hardware products within which the software resides. Business risks include resource availability (both personnel and equipment), cost and budget issues, and schedule milestone completion for market windows and customer delivery.

Within this context of the technological and business perspectives, there are three elements of software risk: technical, cost, and schedule. Each of these software risk elements has a relationship with the other elements, and can be expressed as correlating, or interdependent, factors. For example, from a technological perspective, the three elements entailed in software risk management would occur if a compiler bug appeared during software development. The technical risk is that the software would not execute as expected. This would lead to a cost risk, since unplanned additional effort to either fix the bug or develop a different solution would be required. The additional time taken to develop a solution for the compiler problem (which could affect project milestones) is considered a schedule risk.

From a business perspective, adding personnel can also involve these three elements. The technical risk includes the new people implementing the software incorrectly and not meeting the customers' requirements. The cost risk is the additional cost of the personnel incurred against the budget. The schedule risk involves the new people having a long learning curve and thus missing near-term milestones.

Certain factors and characteristics are associated with risk. Rowe [1] places risk factors for risk valuation and evaluation into the following categories.
- Type of consequence: voluntary/involuntary, immediate/delayed, statistical/identifiable, controlled/uncontrolled.
- Nature of consequence: cultural values, magnitude of consequences, origination of risk event, degree of knowledge.
- Other factors: magnitude of probability, situational factors, psychological behavior of groups and individuals.

Although not directly related to software, the idea of identifying risk factors has merit. Identifying factors describing software characteristics have been used in the past. Research by McCall et al. [2] and Boehm et al. [3] has identified factors related to software quality and reliability. Shumskas [4] and Cooper [5] identified software risk factors from a software procurement perspective. JIT software uses factors to reflect general risk associated with the development of software. These factors encapsulate risks associated with software. Software risk factors identify relationships between the risk elements previously identified in terms of items more closely related to software issues.

As shown in the following figure, a risk factor can relate to more than one risk element. Risk perspectives and risk activities have similar relationships since a risk activity can relate to more than one risk perspective. The table below identifies the software risk factors' influence as it pertains to the software risk elements. Based on industry experience, each risk factor has been given a value of high, medium, or low, identifying its degree of influence on the software risk elements.

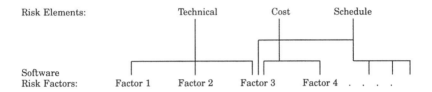

Relationship of Risk Elements to Software Risk Factors

Technical

Technical risks are associated with the performance of the software product. Performance of the software involves the following issues:
- Functionality - The ability of the software to perform to its designed functions.
- Quality - The ability of the software to meet customer expectations.
- Reliability - The ability of the software to execute for extended periods of time without error.
- Usability - The ability of the software and documentation to provide easy implementation of the user requirements.
- Timeliness - The ability of the software to perform the functions in a timely manner.

In some cases it involves:
- Maintainability - The ability of the software and the documentation to be easily maintained by the customer.
- Reusability - The ability of the software to be used again in a similar or different application.

Each of these issues relates to some element of performance risk, although in many cases not equally or not at the same time. The importance of the technical risk issues is determined by the perception of their importance to the customer, to management, and to the developer of the software.

Technical risks are bound by the requirements and design of the software product. That is, the performance issues of the software and the risks associated with meeting customer requirements are related to what is expected by the customer (the requirements), and how these expectations are implemented (the design). Therefore, most risks associated with the technical performance of software are introduced early in the software development life cycle and must be addressed as soon as they are identified.

Purpose
The purpose of this step is to use SERIM metrics to help you calculate your project's Technical risks, and develop action plans to address the low scoring metric questions that increase these risks.

Cost
Cost risks are associated with the cost of the software product during software development, including its final delivery. Cost of the software involves the following issues:
- Budget - The ability to develop software, its associated documentation, and services within a spending limit set by management.
- Nonrecurring Costs - The ability to identify and manage costs associated with the development of the software such as initial development labor and capital equipment.
- Recurring Costs - The ability to identify and manage costs associated with the support of the software development, such as facilities and maintenance costs of software products used in the development.
- Fixed Costs - The ability to identify and manage costs that do not vary, such as the cost of reproduction of software and documentation.
- Variable Costs - The ability to identify and manage costs that vary with the amount of activity of software development, such as rented computer time.

- Profit/Loss Margin - The ability to predict and control the amount of expected profit margin for a product or sale.
- Realism - The ability to project accurate cost based on assumptions given.

Each of these cost issues is associated with the risk of the software product's profit or loss. The identification, assessment, and prediction of cost risks will influence the support and investment management given to the software product.

Cost risks are not bounded until the software product is delivered. Therefore, they exist throughout the software development life cycle. Cost risks are also influenced by other external items, such as the availability of money, the timing of money (when monies are available), and the expectations of the business management.

Purpose
The purpose of this step is to use SERIM metrics to help you calculate your project's Cost risks, and develop action plans to address the low scoring metric questions that increase these risks.

Schedule

Schedule risks are associated with the schedule of the software product during development. The software development schedule involves the following:
- Flexibility - The ability of the schedule to be compressed or extended with expectations of completing the tasks.
- Meeting Established Milestones - The ability of the technical resources to meet the milestones established in a schedule.
- Realism - The ability of the schedule to reflect the expectations of the customers, management, and software developers with accuracy.

Each of these issues can be an influencing factor in the profit/loss or technical performance of the software product. For example, there is usually a correlation between lengthening the schedule and increased development cost. Likewise, a similar correlation appears to exist between shortening the schedule and an increased number of software problems found by the customer, rather than the software development team.

Like cost risks, schedule risks are not bounded until the software product is delivered. Therefore, they exist throughout the software development life cycle. Schedule risks are influenced by other items, such as the availability of equipment and people, funding (that is, starting on internal funds versus customer funds), expansion or change in the scope of the product, and different approaches in software development.

Purpose
The purpose of this step is to use SERIM metrics to help you calculate your project's Schedule risks, and develop action plans to address the low scoring metric questions that increase these risks.

Risk Categories

Certain factors and characteristics are associated with risk. Rowe [1] places risk factors for risk valuation and evaluation into the following categories:
- Type of consequence: voluntary/involuntary, immediate/delayed, statistical/identifiable, controlled/uncontrolled.
- Nature of consequence: cultural values, magnitude of consequences, origination of risk event, degree of knowledge.
- Other factors: magnitude of probability, situational factors, psychological behavior of groups and individuals

Although not directly related to software, the idea of identifying risk factors has merit. Identifying factors describing software characteristics have been used in the past. Research by McCall et al. [2] and Boehm et al. [3] has identified factors related to software quality and reliability. Shumskas [4] and Cooper [5] identified software risk factors from a software procurement perspective. JIT software uses factors to reflect general risk associated with the development of software.

These factors encapsulate risks associated with software. Software risk factors identify relationships between the risk elements previously identified in terms of items more closely related to software issues. Another way to view software risk factors is by their relationship to the software development process or the software product. This influence is identified as either major or minor. Based on industry experience, the terms major and minor reflect the degree of influence that these factors have on the software development process or product.

Software Development Process

There are risks inherent in the software creation process itself. Rating the SERIM Assessment, and then analyzing the metrics from the perspective of the software development process can quantify these risks. Quantifying risks involves analyzing the risk factors that influence the software development process, according to their degree of influence. The following factors have a major influence on the software process:

- Organization – How an organization treats software development through its organization (for example, matrix versus project) will have a major influence on how the software development process is implemented.
- Estimation – Software cost estimation is considered a major influence because the amount of time, shown as schedule and effort, will influence the approach a project will take in its software process. In cases of shorter development time and effort, steps may be omitted. In cases of longer development time with more effort, these steps would be included.
- Monitoring – How well a project is monitored will have a major influence on how well the process is followed. Although the "Hawthorne Effect" was first described 60 years ago, it still influences process implementation today.
- Development Methodology – The choice of development methodology has a major influence on the architecture and approach of the software development process. Development methodologies

vary in expectations regarding adherence, documentation, and reviews of the software.

- Tools – If high-quality tools are used correctly on the project, there will be fewer errors in the product. However, the opposite is also true. Poor-quality tools, or high-quality tools used incorrectly, may also introduce errors into the product.
- Risk Culture – This factor also has a major influence on the software development process. The amount of risk and the tolerance of variability of the process reflect themselves in the software development process.
- Personnel – The amount and type of personnel assigned to a software project will have a significant influence on the process, based on their background, beliefs, thoroughness, and willingness to try new approaches.

Risk factors that have a minor influence on the software process (usually reflected in the product as a result of implementing a software process) include:

- Usability
- Correctness
- Reliability

Purpose

The purpose of this step is to use SERIM metrics to help you calculate your software project's risks related to the software development **Process**, and develop action plans to address the low scoring metric questions that increase these risks.

Software Risk Factors Influence
Against the Software Category Process

SOFTWARE RISK FACTOR	PROCESS
Organization	Major
Estimation	Major
Monitoring	Major
Development Methodology	Major
Tools	Major
Risk Culture	Major
Usability	Minor
Correctness	Minor
Reliability	Minor
Personnel	Major

Software Product

Risks exist even if the software product meets its intended function. The ability to quantify these risks in numeric form allows you to identify which factors influence risk in the product. Of the ten software risk factors, the following have major influence on the software product:

- Tools – If high-quality tools are used correctly on the project, there will be fewer errors in the product. However, the opposite is also true. Poor quality tools, or high-quality tools used incorrectly may also introduce errors in the product.
- Risk Culture – An organization whose culture supports shortchanging the development process to make up for lost time in the schedule will be more likely to produce a product with errors and/or missing requirements.
- Usability – In part, the success of the product will depend on user acceptance. A product that is not user-friendly will have little chance of success, even if it meets the functionality of the user.
- Correctness – Correctness in meeting the customer's requirements and expectations has a major influence on the success of the software product. Missing functionality and/or precision will have a major impact on how well the software meets the customer's needs.
- Reliability – If the software doesn't execute reliably, it will not be successful.

- Personnel – The choice of personnel will have a major influence on the success of the product. The process used (or nor used) by the personnel involved in a software project will have a major effect on the resulting product.

Minor influences (more administrative in nature) on the software product include:
- Organization
- Estimation
- Monitoring
- Development Methodology

Purpose
The purpose of this step is to use SERIM metrics to help you calculate your software project's risks related to the software **Product**, and develop action plans to address the low scoring metric questions that increase these risks.

Software Risk Factors Influence
Against the Software Category Product

SOFTWARE RISK FACTOR	PRODUCT
Organization	Minor
Estimation	Minor
Monitoring	Minor
Development Methodology	Minor
Tools	Major
Risk Culture	Major
Usability	Major
Correctness	Major
Reliability	Major
Personnel	Major

Risk Activities

There are six types of risk activities:

- **Risk Identification** - Involves collecting information about a software development project and classifying it to determine the amount of potential risk to the project.
- **Risk Strategy and Planning** - Involves pursuing the decision alternatives of risk(s) that might occur, and then developing contingency plans for alternatives or for mitigation.
- **Risk Assessment** - Involves determining the effects of potential risks, and making decisions to mitigate, manage, or ignore the risks.
- **Risk Mitigation / Avoidance** - Involves using information gained from the previous activities to avoid risks or minimize their impact.
- **Risk Reporting** - Involves using information gained from the previous activities to compare risk status against previously identified risks.
- **Risk Prediction** - Involves using information gained from the previous activities to forecast risks.

In order to address risks holistically, software management must be viewed from the perspectives previously identified: operational, strategic, technology, business, industry, and practical.

- Operational risks – address the day-to-day uncertainties of a project.
- Strategic risks – identify the long-term effects on a company.
- Technology risks – are associated with the use of software technology.
- Business risks – of software affect a company's projects in a variety of ways.
- Industry risks – address the view of industry software development models and processes.
- Practical risks – relate to the implementation of software practices.

As you progress through the steps in this module, all of the risk management activities are analyzed according to the previously mentioned perspectives.

An Assessment of Proposed Software Risk Management Activities
Against Different Risk Perspectives

RISK ACTIVITIES	RISK PERSPECTIVES					
	Oper.	Strat.	Tech.	Bus.	Indst.	Pract.
Risk Identification	31	31	31	31	31	32
Risk Strategy & Planning	32	32	32	32	33	33
Risk Assessment	33	33	33	33	34	34
Risk Mitigation & Avoidance	34	34	35	35	35	35
Risk Reporting	35	35	36	36	36	36
Risk Prediction	36	36	37	37	37	37

Oper = Operational, Strat = Strategic, Tech = Technical,
Bus = Business, Indst = Industry, Pract = Practitioner

This table compares the six risk activities identified for software risk management with the six risk perspectives. By addressing each relationship, awareness is gained of the importance of these risk relationships, which are not found in previous software management practices.

Some of these activities are built upon previous activities. For example, you cannot assess or mitigate risks without first identifying them. You also cannot predict risks without finding out the status of previously identified risks.

Risk Identification

The activity of identifying software risks answers these questions:
- Is there risk involved in this activity?
- How can it be classified?

Identifying software risks involves collecting information about the software development project and classifying it to determine the amount of potential risk to the project. Information gathering encompasses identifying past and current information. There are six methods and sources of gathering risk information [11], [12]:

- traditional or folk knowledge
- analogies to well-known cases
- common sense assessments
- results of experiments or tests
- reviews of inadvertent exposure
- epidemiological surveys

Traditional or folk knowledge is perceived information; it may, or may not, be real. Stereotypes fall within this category. For example, traditional or folk knowledge for software perceives embedded software development as being more complex, and thereby more risky than applications-based software. Depending on the case, there may be some truth to this perception. In other cases, such as more complex distributed application systems, this perception may not be true.

Analogies to well-known cases relate types of activities showing similar traits. Analogies are based on historical data, past lesson-learned reports, or past personal experiences on projects. An example of analogies to well-known cases may be reviewing past or current software productivity figures against a development language or a new development environment. Analogies are commonly used in the software engineering profession, since they are an easy means of providing rationale about risks.

Common sense assessments are based on judgments rooted in past experience and current knowledge. There is usually no data to substantiate the risk identification and resulting action. For example, determining the person who could lead a team of software engineers to develop a product or a subsystem is usually based on personal judgment of prior activities.

Results of experiments or tests involve a process of "buying" information to confirm the identification of risks. The purpose is to help reduce the uncertainty of the risk situation by gaining more data. An example of this would be performing a small design task on several new CASE tools in order to better assess their capabilities before committing to one that will be used to produce a software product.

Reviews of inadvertent exposure are commonly used in the software development process once a user has the software. It involves using the software in ways not thought of or originally intended. An example of this type of information is the early use of some software-based telephone switches with "undocumented" features, allowing subscribers to place calls without being charged by flashing the hook switch a certain way.

Epidemiological surveys provide information by collecting data from a large population. This provides information by inference, and relates a cause to an observed effect. An example are surveys of potential customers who respond to different ways user-interface software can be implemented and their opinions about them. As previously mentioned, risk identification has different meanings based on the following six perceptions and how they relate to the use of risk information.

The operational perspective reviews data associated with the risk of the software project. Operational risk identification includes reviewing metrics on project schedule, costs, or technical parameters such as percent processor utilization.

The strategic perspective identifies data associated with future risks of the business. Examples include schedule data relating software products in order to capture market windows, projected profit/loss effects of software projects, and the evaluation of software technology maturity for future projects.

The technical perspective identifies risks associated with implementing software technology on a project. This can comprise examples which include developing software with an unproven compiler, using a new programming language or design methodology, and identifying critical timing relationships between software-to-software or software-to-hardware modules.

The business perspective identifies the impact of a software product on the business operations. Examples of this include the impact of late deliveries to the customer, warranty costs due to latent defects, and the cost of additional computer capital to perform the software development task.

The industry perspective associates risks with the software development models used in industry. Included in this perspective are the general risks associated with design, coding, or the testing process.

The practical perspective identifies risks from the software developers' point of view. Examples of this include risks associated with eliminating extra tests in order to meet the schedule, not checking the code against the design to ensure that all the design features have been incorporated, and the risk that the target hardware for which the software was written does not change.

Purpose
The purpose of this step is to use SERIM metrics to help you identify your software project's risks, and develop action plans to address the low scoring metric questions from the following perspectives:
- Operational
- Strategic
- Technical
- Business
- Industry
- Practical

Risk Strategy and Planning

Strategizing and planning for software risks based on risk identification information involves pursuing the decision alternatives of risk(s) that might occur, and then developing contingency plans for alternatives or for mitigation. The resulting plans then set the direction for managing risks during the development of software. Like risk identification, risk strategy and planning has been evaluated according to the six perspectives of risk management.

The operational perspective involves planning activities related to the software project. Planning risk mitigation to obtain resources such as a project's staffing profile or software tool availability is one example of this activity

The strategic perspective involves planning related to the company's long-term objectives. Examples of this include investing in new software technology such as expert systems, or entering a new market that involves software development never previously performed in the company.

The technical perspective pertains to the tools and implementation of the software. Examples of risk strategy and planning from this technical perspective include learning a new computer language or identifying the development of complex algorithms.

The business perspective plans the impact of software from a profit and loss view. An example of this type of planning includes decisions on what software features to offer based on the competition or potential revenue (or future losses) of additional software functionality.

The industry perspective involves implementation of new software development processes. Examples of this involve implementing object-oriented analysis and design or the use of cleanroom software development.

The practical perspective involves the implementation risks as viewed by the software developer. The identification of requirements and the stability of target hardware platforms are examples of this type of risk planning.

Purpose
The purpose of this step is to use SERIM metrics to help you develop risk strategies and plans for your project based on the risks you identified in the previous step, from the following perspectives:
- Operational
- Strategic
- Technical
- Business

- Industry
- Practical

Risk Assessment

The activity of assessing software risks involves the process of determining the effects of potential risk areas. Risk assessment involves asking questions such as: Is this a risk or not? How serious is the risk? What are the consequences? What is the likelihood of this risk happening? Decisions are made based on the risk being assessed. The decision(s) may be to mitigate, manage, or ignore the risks depending on the influence of the following six perspectives.

The operational perspective allows the assessment of risks from an overall project viewpoint. Examples of operational risk assessment include the identification of the correct person performing the right task (a cost and technical quality risk), or the assessment of the integration risks with another software product.

The strategic perspective assesses risks from a total business viewpoint. Examples of this include the decision to upgrade all the software products to a new operating system (costs incurred) versus future sales based on this feature, or the decision to move into a new product area even if it means taking away resources from committed projects.

The technical perspective determines technical implementation risks. Upgrading a compiler (knowledge of past bugs and their fixes versus the delays in finding and fixing new bugs), or risking the addition of a new feature in software without fully testing it, are examples of software technical risks.

The business perspective evaluates profit, loss, and the competition factors. Software risk assessment examples include delaying shipment of the software to improve the quality (immediate lost sales versus future lost sales), or the decision to delay implementing a new software feature based on the competitors' perceived marketing strategy.

The industry perspective estimates the risks associated with new processes. The trade-off in time and errors involved in using a prototyping methodology, or implementing software designs from bottom-up versus top-down approach are prime examples of industrial software risk assessments.

The practical perspective revolves around the software developers' viewpoint. Examples of assessing software risks from this perspective include the likelihood of additional training on a tool (reducing or slipping a milestone), or the probability that performing regression testing on a unit of code will not find any additional errors.

Purpose
The purpose of this step is to use SERIM metrics to help you determine the effects of potential risks, from the following perspectives.
- Operational
- Strategic
- Technical
- Business
- Industry
- Practical

Risk Mitigation

The activity of mitigating and avoiding software risks is based on the information gained from the previous activities of identifying, planning, and assessing risks. Software risk mitigation/avoidance activities avoid risks or minimize their impact. Risks are viewed as having a negative impact on the activity being performed. These views and their perspectives are outlined in the following paragraphs.

The operational perspective relates mitigation risk to the overall viewpoint of the project. Using extra software development personnel on a project to reduce schedule risks because of the lack of resources, or the need to have different vendors build the same product to reduce large schedule or quality variability are examples of risk mitigation/avoidance.

Mitigating risks from a total business viewpoint is another tool in risk mitigation/avoidance from a strategic perspective. Hiring an outside consultant to review the software development process and progress on many projects, having outside vendors perform software development based on their successful track-record, and the use of contract clauses are tools used to achieve this purpose.

From a technical perspective, risks that affect the technical performance of the software must be mitigated. Not upgrading an emulator and working with one that is well known and debugged, or staying with a well-proven software design methodology that requires minimal training are examples of software risk mitigation.

Minimizing loss, such as a loss of schedule or loss of profit, addresses mitigation/avoidance from a business perspective. Establishing solid software requirements in order to avoid rework or inviting the customer to assist in the development of the software to gain a higher probability of acceptance are steps used to minimize loss.

The industry perspective of mitigation risks is associated with the software development process. Using inspections and walkthroughs to mitigate errors or using traceability techniques to ensure that all software features are tested are examples of this activity.

In the practical perspective, risk mitigation/avoidance involves the viewpoint of a software developer. This step includes additional software tool or language training to mitigate additional cost and schedule slip, or the early identification of technical problems to minimize any potential cost or schedule consequences at a later date.

Purpose
The purpose of this step is to use SERIM metrics to help you develop methods to mitigate/avoid risks in developing your project, from the following perspectives:
- Operational
- Strategic
- Technical
- Business

- Industry
- Practical

Risk Reporting

Risk reporting is based on information obtained from the previous topics (those of identifying, planning, assessing, and mitigating risks). It involves comparing risk status against previously identified risks. These are explained in the following paragraphs.

Examples of the operational perspective on risk reporting in the context of a software project include:
1. A vendor delivering a software product late
2. A project budget based on risks previously identified

The strategic perspective involves reporting risks from a company viewpoint. Examples include comparing risk information previously identified against gaining market share, or introducing a new software product line.

The technical perspective encompasses risk reporting that may affect the technical performance of the software. This includes reporting risks such as limited internal memory size, or limitations of response time.

The business perspective involves reporting risks that may affect the profit/loss, schedule, or the competition. Examples of this aspect include communicating the risks that affect profit margins, or the impact the competition will have on sales based on the early introduction of its software product.

The industry perspective involves reporting risks that affect the software development process. Examples of this include the quality of software based on a new software development methodology, or the results of errors (based on the use of regression testing) found after delivery.

The practical perspective involves reporting risks from a software developers' viewpoint. This includes reporting risks because of increased time in learning a new software development tool, or risks associated with problems found in the target hardware.

Purpose
The purpose of this step is to use SERIM metrics to help you compare your project's risk status against previously identified risks, from the following perspectives:
- Operational
- Strategic
- Technical
- Business
- Industry
- Practical

Risk Prediction

Risk prediction is derived from the previous activities of identifying, planning, assessing, mitigating, and reporting risks. Software risk prediction involves forecasting risks using the history and knowledge of previously identified risks. Using the following six perspectives further clarifies risk prediction.

The operational perspective predicts risks that relate to a project. Examples of risk prediction include assessing the probability of going over-budget based on the rate of current and predicted expenditures, or assessing the probability of meeting the next project milestone on time.

The strategic perspective predicts risks that relate to a business. Predicting the risk of the failure of bringing a new product line to market, or predicting the risks associated with investment in new software technology are examples of this type of activity.

The technical perspective involves predicting risks associated with the technical performance of the product. Examples of this activity include predicting the reliability risks of software, or predicting the risk of missing requirements when the software is delivered to the customer.

From the business perspective, predicting risks is associated with budget, schedule, or the competition. Examples of this aspect include predicting the risk of late delivery schedule, or the loss of sales to the competition based on their introduction of a new feature.

The industry perspective involves predicting risks associated with the software development process. Examples of this include predicting the risk of additional errors, time, or budget by skipping steps in the software development process.

The practical perspective involves predicting risks from a software developers' viewpoint. Examples of this perspective include predicting the risk of completing the software task based on the development environment, or predicting the risk of making the software timing or memory budgets based on the implementation task.

Purpose
The purpose of this step is to use SERIM metrics to help you predict your project's risks, from the following perspectives:
- Operational
- Strategic
- Technical
- Business
- Industry
- Practical

Development Phases

- **Pre-Requirements** - Involves analyzing risks associated with project cost, schedule and staffing estimations, personnel availability, and project monitoring structure.

- **Requirements** - Involves analyzing risks associated with project organization, functional and performance requirements definition, and performance trade-offs.
- **Design** - Involves analyzing risks associated with functionality implementation, the flow of requirements into design, and design methodology implementation.
- **Coding** - Involves analyzing risks associated with functionality implementation, requirements flowing from design concept into code, and error handling implementation.
- **Testing** - Involves analyzing risks associated with flowing the requirements and design concept into test plans and procedures, regression testing, and software reliability estimation.
- **Delivery and Maintenance** - Involves analyzing risks associated with logging and completing customer problems, enhancing the software with new features, and planning adequate help for the user.

A methodology lays the groundwork identifying the steps needed to perform a task. An integrated software risk management methodology identifies the steps, or phases, taken to manage software risks across the software development life cycle. Just-In-Time (JIT) software is an integrated software risk management methodology, which is derived from several perspectives. JIT methodology links these perspectives to each software development phase by correlating appropriate projects to the following risk management activities: risk identification, risk strategy and planning, risk assessment, risk mitigation/avoidance, risk reporting, and risk prediction. The following figure identifies the six phases to be performed during the life cycle of software development in order to manage risk. These phases are pre-requirements, requirements, design, code, test, delivery, and maintenance. Over time, risk activities related to the individual phases flow across the software development life cycle and down to the next phase, creating additional information that would be used to manage risk activities.

In the following sections, the six risk activities are further explored and explained according to the phases of the software development life cycle. Within the context of each phase, the risk activities are also evaluated by using the metric method. The metric questions in this chapter use the same abbreviations to refer to the following 10 risk factors: organization (O), estimation (E), monitoring (M), development methodology (DM), tools (T), risk culture (RC), usability (U), correctness (C), reliability (R), and personnel (P). Viewed holistically, these life cycle phases comprise JIT software.

The following table summarizes the software risk metric questions that were applied to the different phases of the software development life cycle.

Identification of Software Development Life Cycle Phases
Against Metric Questions

Metric Question	Pre-Requirements	Requirements	Design	Coding	Testing	Delivery & Maintenance
O1	X	X	X	X	X	X
O2	X					
O3	X	X	X	X	X	X
O4	X	X	X	X	X	X
O5	X	X	X	X	X	X
O6		X	X	X	X	X
O7		X	X	X	X	X
O8		X	X	X	X	X
E1	X					
E2	X					
E3	X					
E4	X					
E5		X	X	X	X	X
E6	X	X	X	X	X	X
E7	X	X	X	X	X	X
M1	X					
M2	X					
M3	X	X	X	X	X	X
M4	X	X	X	X	X	X
M5		X	X	X	X	X
M6	X	X	X	X	X	X
M7	X	X	X	X	X	X

Metric Question	Pre-Requirements	Requirements	Design	Coding	Testing	Delivery & Maintenance
D1	X					
D2	X	X	X	X	X	X
D3		X	X	X	X	X
D4		X	X	X		
D5					X	
D6	X	X	X	X	X	X
D7					X	
T1	X	X	X	X	X	X
T2			X			
T3					X	
T4					X	
T5					X	
T6	X	X	X	X	X	X
T7						X
T8				X		
T9	X	X	X	X	X	X
RC1	X	X	X	X	X	X
RC2	X	X	X	X	X	X
RC3	X	X	X	X	X	X
RC4	X	X	X	X	X	X
RC5	X	X	X	X	X	X
RC6	X	X	X	X	X	X
RC7	X					
RC8	X					
RC9	X					
RC10	X					
RC11	X					
U1						X
U2		X	X	X	X	X
U3		X				
U4			X			
U5		X				

Metric Question	Pre-Requirements	Requirements	Design	Coding	Testing	Delivery & Maintenance
U6			X			
C1		X				
C2			X			
C3				X		
C4					X	
C5	X	X	X	X	X	X
C6				X		
C7					X	
C8						X
C9					X	
R1			X	X		
R2			X	X		
R3		X	X	X		
R4				X		
R5			X	X		
R6				X		
R7					X	
R8						X
R9					X	
R10					X	
R11					X	
R12					X	
P1	X					
P2	X					
P3	X					
P4	X					
P5	X					

Pre-Requirements

Example of activities within the pre-requirements phase include project cost, schedule and staffing estimation, personnel availability, and project monitoring structure. Since decisions made at this phase of the software life cycle affect the rest of the project, the risk impacts of these decisions are significant.

Because this phase deals more with conceptual approaches and solutions, a way to rank various options is to use a technique called Quality Function Deployment (QFD) [13]. QFD identifies the functions the customer is interested in (the "whats") and the different approaches to the solution (the "hows"). This is placed in a matrix form, as shown in the following figure.

QFD Approach in Identifying the Best Software Concept

WHAT	WEIGHT	ALT1	ALT2	ALT3	COMMENTS
HOW					
User Friendly	3	5	1	3	Some Training Required
Runs On A PC	5	5	3	1	Customer-Owned Equipment
Query Language	4	3	3	5	Wants To Sort Records
Reports	3	3	5	5	Screens Rather Than Printed
.	.	.	.	.	.
.	.	.	.	.	.
.	.	.	.	.	.
TOTAL		305	296	320	

The concept of QFD identifies the best software alternative approach that meets the customers' functions. To begin filling in the QFD matrix, first list the major software functions (taken from the customers' perspective) under the column headed "What." A function weight of 1 (least important) to 5 (most important) is then assigned to each software function.

The next column heading identifies the alternative approaches under consideration. Using the figure as an example, Alternative Approach 1 may be using several different PC packages and encapsulating them under an executive program. Alternative Approach 2 may be workstation software that performs similar functions but has to be expanded to include new functionality. Alternative Approach 3 may be a mainframe application that has to be rewritten for a PC environment.

The power of the QFD is realized in how it can be used. The values in each column cell can have a rating of 5 (meets the criteria), 3 (meets some of the criteria), and 1 (meets little of the criteria). A zero value is used if it does not meet any of the criteria. So what are the criteria?

The criteria can be anything you want them to be. For example, in the figure above, the criterion being considered could be cost. In this case, 5 means it can meet cost constraints. A value of 1 means it is not very likely to meet cost constraints. By multiplying the function weight and the numeric rating under each column, and then adding the resulting values for each column, you can calculate a total score. The column with the highest score has the best chance for achieving customer functionality.

Other criteria to consider are schedule and technical performance. By adding the resulting total score for each alternative for cost, schedule, and technical performance, a final composite score is calculated. This score identifies which alternative approach would have the best chance for achieving customer functionality, with the least risks.

As previously mentioned, software risk management questions can measure the activity risks of the software project. The following table identifies the software risk metric questions appropriate for measuring risk activities within the pre-requirements phase.

Identification of Risk Activities
Against Metric Questions In the Pre-Requirements Phase

Metric Question	Risk Activities					
	Identification	Strategy / Planning	Assessment	Mitigation/ Avoidance	Reporting	Prediction
O1	X		X	X		X
O2	X		X			X

Metric Question	Risk Activities					
	Identification	Strategy / Planning	Assessment	Mitigation/ Avoidance	Reporting	Prediction
O3	X	X	X	X		X
O4	X					X
O5	X					X
E1	X	X				X
E2	X	X	X	X		X
E3	X	X	X	X		X
E4	X	X	X	X		X
E6	X	X	X			X
E7	X	X	X			X
M1	X	X		X		X
M2	X			X	X	X
M3	X			X	X	X
M4	X			X	X	X
M6	X		X	X	X	X
M7	X		X	X	X	X
D1	X	X		X		X
D2	X			X		X
D6	X			X		X
T1	X			X		X
T6	X		X			X
T9	X					X
RC1	X					X
RC2	X					X
RC3	X					X
RC4	X					X
RC5	X					X
RC6	X					X
RC7	X					X
RC8	X					X
RC9	X					X
RC10	X			X		X

Metric Question	Risk Activities					
	Identification	Strategy / Planning	Assessment	Mitigation/ Avoidance	Reporting	Prediction
RC11	X	X		X		X
C5	X		X			X
P1	X	X	X	X		X
P2	X			X		X
P3	X			X		X
P4	X			X		X
P5	X					X

Questions in the Pre-Requirements Phase

The answers to these metric questions can be used to clarify the impact the six risk management activities have on the pre-requirements phase of software development. In the following paragraphs, these risks are presented in a series of six steps. Each step builds upon the other. In each step, the risk activity is identified, followed by a list of metric questions that relate to that particular activity.

1. Risk identification - All of the metric questions influence the rest of the software development life cycle.
2. Risk strategy and planning which involves developing new and contingency plans: O3, E1, E2, E3, E4, E6, E7, M1, D1, RC11, and P1.
3. Risk assessment, or determining what the effect is in each area of risk: O1, O2, O3, E2, E3, E4, E6, E7, M6, M7, T6, and P1.
4. Mitigation/avoidance: O1, O3, E2, E3, E4, M1, M2, M3, M4, M6, M7, D1, D2, D6, T1, RC10, RC11, P1, P2, P3, and P4.
5. Risk reporting, or communicating known risks in a timely manner: M2, M3, M4, M6, and M7.
6. Risk prediction: this must occur so that future risks are avoided. Answering all of the metric questions helps to identify the potential areas of risk and the possible improvements to reduce those risks.

Purpose

The purpose of this step is to help you generate the SERIM metrics required to calculate your project's risk in the PRE-REQUIREMENTS phase of development. You can then examine the risk metrics applicable to each of the six risk management activities, identify specific areas of risk derived from the metric questions, and develop action plans to manage these risks.

Requirements

Project organization, definition of functional and performance requirements, and performance trade-offs are examples of activities within the requirements phase. Since decisions made at this phase of the software life cycle affect the rest of the project, the risk impact of these decisions is also significant. A requirement specification translates the customer's expectations into a document from which the software developers can start designing. In many cases, misinterpretation of the intent (behavioral and non-behavioral expectations) of the requirement specifications occurs. Hopefully, these misinterpretations are found later in the software development life cycle. One way to reduce these risks is to develop a software prototype or model.

A prototype allows software developers to take conceptual ideas identified in software requirements and translate them into design and implementation details. For example, a user-interface intensive software product requirement may only define the functionality (the "whats") the system should perform. A prototype could take many of the requirements and demonstrate both the non-behaviorial aspects (such as screen layout, colors used, icon choices, and report formats), and the behavioral aspects of the software (such as how the screens are tied together, or the choices made to use a mouse or keyboard for input). In this context, a prototype is called an *executable* requirement, as opposed to a *written* requirement.

A model is another form of executable requirement. The purpose of a software model is to represent implementation functionality by exploring algorithms and interfaces (such as protocols) that are identified as risks. Addressing these algorithms and interfaces (or risks) is a part of the unknown implementation approach, and decisions regarding these risks correspond to the future changes made in the software. This can significantly affect the algorithms and interfaces later in the development life cycle. Besides implementation functionality, behavioral implementation issues such as timing, throughput, and data storage can also be modeled.

Prototypes, models, and other forms of executable requirements only supplement the customer's written requirements—they do not replace them. The advantage of executable requirements is that it reduces the risk of improper implementation of customer requirements by interpreting the intent of the requirements early, thereby avoiding effort later in the development life cycle when changes are more costly and will have a major impact on the schedule. Prototypes and models can also be reviewed by other software developers and the customer to verify the approach and the ''look-and-feel'' of the software while it is still early in its development cycle. Modifications can be made at this point without any substantial increase in effort and schedule. The investment up-front for executable requirements more than offset the investment later on in the development life cycle. Executable requirements also have additional benefits, such as less decision-making later in design, a better sense of how the finished software product should look and/or execute, possible reuse of code if planned properly and using the right tools, and an earlier start of a more complete users manual, test plans and procedures. The following figure shows the difference between the development flow with written requirements only, and with the use of written and executable requirements.

WRITTEN REQUIREMENTS ONLY - REAL-LIFE FLOW

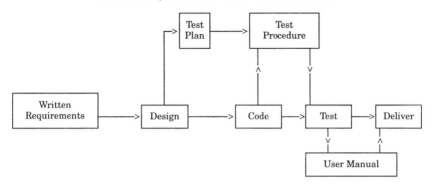

WRITTEN AND EXECUTABLE REQUIREMENT - NEW FLOW

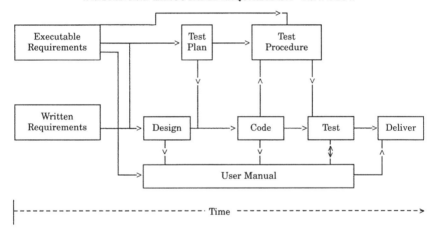

Differences In Software Development Flow With Use and
Non-Use of Executable Software Requirements

This figure shows that the executable requirements feed into many of the software development activities that, in turn, allow many of the activities to start earlier and with more complete information. Using executable requirements can lead to the following results.

Risk areas are found and addressed earlier in the life cycle, which helps to reduce negative consequences to schedule, cost, and technical performance. Developers work more development activities in parallel, thus saving schedule to produce software just-in-time. Less effort is required later in the project's life cycle, since the majority of the work was done earlier. This leads to better schedule time-frames and higher confidence in the quality of the software prior to delivery.

The two approaches also have different effects on staffing and expenditure of hours. Executable requirements expend more effort in the process earlier, because more parallel development is related to identifying and fixing problems earlier in the life cycle. As a result, the total overall effort is decreased, and the schedule is shorter.

To identify and assess requirement risks, metrics must be obtained. Within the context of the requirements phase, the software risk metric questions within the table below are appropriate to measure the six risk activities.

Identification of Risk Activities Against
Metric Questions in the Requirements Phase

Metric Question	Risk Activities					
	Identification	Strategy / Planning	Assessment	Mitigation/ Avoidance	Reporting	Prediction
O1	X		X	X		X
O3	X	X	X	X		X
O4	X					X
O5	X					X
O6	X			X		X
O7	X		X	X		X
O8	X		X	X		X
E5	X	X	X	X	X	X
E6	X	X	X			X
E7	X	X	X			X
M3	X			X	X	X
M4	X			X	X	X
M5	X		X	X	X	X
M6	X		X	X	X	X

Metric Question	Risk Activities					
	Identification	Strategy / Planning	Assessment	Mitigation/ Avoidance	Reporting	Prediction
M7	X		X	X	X	X
D2	X			X		X
D3	X		X			X
D4	X			X		X
D6	X			X		X
T1	X			X		X
T6	X		X			X
T9	X					X
RC1	X					X
RC2	X					X
RC3	X					X
RC4	X					X
RC5	X					X
RC6	X					X
U2	X					X
U3	X		X	X		X
U5	X			X		X
C1	X		X	X		X
C5	X		X			X
R3	X		X			X

Questions in the Requirements Phase

The answers to these metric questions can be used to clarify the impact the six risk management activities have on the requirements phase of software development. In the following paragraphs, these risks are presented in a series of six steps. Each step builds upon the other. In each step, the risk activity is identified, followed by a list of metric questions that relate to that particular activity.

1. Risk identification: all of the metric questions need to be used in order to show the influence of this activity on the requirements and following phases of the software development life cycle.

2. Risk strategy and planning, which involves planning new and contingency plans: O3, E5, E6, and E7.
3. Risk assessment, or determining what the effect is on each area of risk: O1, O3, O7, O8, E5, E6, E7, M5, M6, M7, D3, T6, U3, C1, C5, and R3.
4. Mitigation/avoidance: O1, O3, O6, O7, O8, E5, M3, M4, M5, M6, M7, D2, D4, D6, T1, U3, U5, and C1.
5. Risk reporting, or communicating known risks in a timely manner: E5, M3, M4, M5, M6, and M7.
6. Risk prediction must occur so that future risks are avoided. Risk predictions identify potential risk areas to direct ways of possible improvement so future risks can be avoided. In order to obtain the best information for this activity, all of the metric questions need to be used.

Purpose
The purpose of this step is to help you generate the SERIM metrics required to calculate your project's risk in the REQUIREMENTS phase of development. You can then examine the risk metrics applicable to each of the six risk management activities, identify specific areas of risk derived from the metric questions, and develop action plans to manage these risks.

Design

Decisions regarding functionality implementation, requirements flow into design, and design methodology implementation are all part of the design phase. Since decisions made at this phase of the software life cycle affect the code, test, delivery and maintenance phases, the risk impacts of the decisions made during this phase are still important.

The potential approaches to software design range from structured to object-based, with many variations in-between. To reduce risks by identifying design issues early, the following activities should be performed with the software design methodology chosen. It is important to continue prototyping and modeling efforts started during software requirements. As stated earlier, this will identify issues, like human-interface design, or other items that you want to prototype or model. Develop a top-layer, breath-wide architecture. This will help identify structural interfaces between subsystems, and start the process of developing a data dictionary. Develop a depth-functional branch of the design, so that issues related to protocol, timing, and data storage are identified early in the design process. This will also allow coding to begin earlier in the design process.

Measuring risk during the design of the software allows you to better manage the rest of the software development process. The following table identifies the software risk metric questions that are appropriate for measuring the six risk activities within the context of the design phase.

Identification of Risk Activities
Against Metric Questions in the Design Phase

Metric Quest	Identification	Strategy / Planning	Assessment	Mitigation/ Avoidance	Reporting	Prediction
			Risk Activities			
O1	X		X	X		X
O3	X	X	X	X		X
O4	X					X
O5	X					X
O6	X			X		X
O7	X		X	X		X
O8	X		X	X		X
E5	X	X	X	X	X	X
E6	X	X	X			X
E7	X	X	X			X
M3	X			X	X	X
M4	X			X	X	X
M5	X		X	X	X	X
M6	X		X	X	X	X
M7	X		X	X	X	X
D2	X			X		X
D3	X		X			X

Metric Quest	Risk Activities					
	Identification	Strategy / Planning	Assessment	Mitigation/ Avoidance	Reporting	Prediction
D4	X			X		X
D6	X			X		X
T1	X			X		X
T2	X		X			X
T6	X		X			X
T9	X					X
RC1	X					X
RC2	X					X
RC3	X					X
RC4	X					X
RC5	X					X
RC6	X					X
U2	X					X
U4	X		X			X
U6	X		X			X
C2	X		X	X		X
C5	X		X			X
R1	X		X			X
R2	X					X
R3	X		X			X
R5	X		X			X

Questions in the Design Phase

The answers to these metric questions can be used to clarify the impact the six risk management activities have on the design phase of software development. In the following paragraphs, these risks are presented in a series of six steps. Each step builds upon the other. In each step, the risk activity is identified, followed by a list of metric questions that relate to that particular activity.

1. Risk identification, or risks that may affect the design and following phases of the software development life cycle. All of the metric questions should be used.

2. Risk strategy and planning, or developing new and contingency plans: O3, E5, E6, and E7.
3. Risk assessment, or evaluating what the effect is of each area of risk: O1, O3, O7, O8, E5, E6, E7, M5, M6, M7, D3, T2, T6, U4, U6, C2, C5, R1, R3, and R5.
4. Mitigation/avoidance: O1, O3, O6, O7, O8, E5, M3, M4, M5, M6, M7, D2, D4, D6, T1, and C2.
5. Risk reporting, or addressing the known risks: E5, M3, M4, M5, M6, and M7.
6. Predicting risks: all of the metric questions applicable to the design phase should be used. Viewed together, these questions can determine which potential areas of risk can be designated for possible improvements so that future risks can be avoided.

Purpose

The purpose of this step is to help you generate the SERIM metrics required to calculate your project's risk in the DESIGN phase of development. You can then examine the risk metrics applicable to each of the six risk management activities, identify specific areas of risk derived from the metric questions, and develop action plans to manage these risks.

Code

Functionality implementation, requirements flowing from design concept into code, error handling implementation, and so forth, are example activities of the code phase. Since decisions made at this phase of the software life cycle affect the test, delivery, and maintenance phases, the risk impacts of the decisions made during this phase are still important.

Code implementation is one of the most straightforward process activities during the software development life cycle. The following figure illustrates the process for starting coding after your design is complete, so you do not have to do it again.

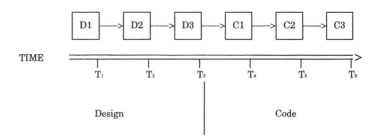

Design First Then Code Implementation

As experienced software developers, you know that the implementation of the code affects the design in the same way the design affects implementation of the code. Because this is known, you want to find out during the design phase what implementation issues will affect the design prior to its completion. This means that planning design and coding need to be done in parallel.

Performing design and code in parallel has several advantages. First, it identifies the differences and gaps between the design documentation detail and what is required for code implementation early in this phase. Reviewing the design creates the impetus for certain types of implementation questions that start with "How do I get from here to ... ?" or "What does this mean?" or "Where do I find ... ?" Most projects have these types of questions that require the design to be modified or supplemented with additional information.

Second, it allows the development team to verify the tools for implementation early, like the compiler, linker, and so forth. By working with the tools early, the software developers can start to identify the tools' limitations and problems, allowing them to change to accommodate their design approach to fit their findings if the tools cannot be completely fixed. This helps prevent a major rework in design by uncovering these limitations before the design is completed.

Comparing the two figures illustrates the third advantage: the parallel development approach takes less time to complete. In order to implement this approach correctly, it requires additional management attention, but with the use of PERT (Programming Evaluation and Review Technique) charts to plan and track these activities, it is not an extraordinary effort and can easily replace the GANTT charts most people have to maintain anyway.

It is important to identify risks early. For measuring the risk associated with the code phase, the following table contains the software risk metric questions you need to consider.

Identification of Risk Activities
Against Metric Questions in the Code Phase.

Metric Question	Risk Activities					
	Identification	Strategy / Planning	Assessment	Mitigation/ Avoidance	Reporting	Prediction
O1	X		X	X		X
O3	X	X	X	X		X
O4	X					X
O5	X					X
O6	X			X		X
O7	X		X	X		X
O8	X		X	X		X
E5	X	X	X	X	X	X
E6	X	X	X			X
E7	X	X	X			X
M3	X			X	X	X
M4	X			X	X	X
M5	X		X	X	X	X
M6	X		X	X	X	X
M7	X		X	X	X	X
D2	X			X		X
D3	X		X			X

Metric Question	Risk Activities					
	Identification	Strategy / Planning	Assessment	Mitigation/ Avoidance	Reporting	Prediction
D4	X			X		X
D6	X			X		X
T1	X			X		X
T6	X		X			X
T8	X					X
T9	X					X
RC1	X					X
RC2	X					X
RC3	X					X
RC4	X					X
RC5	X					X
RC6	X					X
U2	X					X
C3	X		X	X		X
C5	X		X			X
C6	X		X	X		X
R1	X		X			X
R2	X					X
R3	X		X			X
R4	X		X			X
R5	X		X			X
R6	X		X			X

Questions in the Code Phase

The answers to these metric questions can be used to clarify the impact the six risk management activities have on the code phase of software development. In the following paragraphs, these risks are presented in a series of six steps. Each step builds upon the other. In each step, the risk activity is identified, followed by a list of metric questions that relate to that particular activity.

1. Risk identification, or risks that may affect the code and following phases of the software development life cycle. All of the metric questions that apply to the code phase should be used.
2. Risk strategy and planning: O3, E5, E6, and E7.
3. Risk assessment: O1, O3, O7, O8, E5, E6, E7, M5, M6, M7, D3, T6, C3, C5, C6, R1, R3, R4, R5, and R6.
4. Mitigation/avoidance: O1, O3, O6, O7, E5, M3, M4, M5, M6, M7, D2, D4, D6, T1, C3, and C6.
5. Risk reporting: E5, M3, M4, M5, M6, and M7.
6. Predicting risks: All of the metric questions that apply to the code phase should be used in order to identify potential areas of risks and to suggest possible improvements to avoid future risks.

Purpose
The purpose of this step is to help you generate the SERIM metrics required to calculate your project's risk in the CODE phase of development. You can then examine the risk metrics applicable to each of the six risk management activities, identify specific areas of risk derived from the metric questions, and develop action plans to manage these risks.

Test

The test phase includes flowing the requirements and design concept into test plans and procedures, regression testing, and software reliability estimation. Since decisions made at this phase of the software life cycle affect the delivery and maintenance phase, the risk impacts of the decisions made during this phase are reflected in the final product. Testing, as practiced by most organizations, is commonly performed as a sequential series of tests.

A way to shorten the testing cycle and to identify risks early is to perform step-wise cumulative acceptance testing. This approach "sells" the software by incremental functionality (depth functional branch) during the development of code. As each software function is coded/unit tested, it goes through an integration test to verify the functionality. In order to verify it completely, the first software build most likely will include some scaffolding around the functionality.

After integration testing, the functional software package is then subjected to formal acceptance testing with test procedures, user manuals, and other needed items. At this point the software is residing on the deliverable hardware. Once the functionality is tested and accepted, the code is put under a configuration-controlled library, and is frozen until it is delivered to the customer. This process continues for each function (or a group of functions) with each functional build adding on to the previous one. At each software integration test, regression testing is performed on the previous accepted functionality to verify that the new functionality added did not affect the code that was accepted. If the code has to be witness tested, or accepted by the customer, the customer will attend each of the acceptance tests. Because of schedule pressures, if a partial delivery of functionality has to be made, the library should contain fully verified and validated software (placed under configuration control) that could be shipped.

Along with step-wise cumulative testing, the following table contains the software risk metric questions appropriate for measuring the six risk activities that relate to the test phase.

Identification of Risk Activities Against Metric Questions in the Test Phase.

Metric Quest	Risk Activities					
	Identification	Strategy / Planning	Assessment	Mitigation/ Avoidance	Reporting	Prediction
O1	X		X	X		X
O3	X	X	X	X		X
O4	X					X
O5	X					X
O6	X			X		X
O7	X		X	X		X
O8	X		X	X		X
E5	X	X	X	X	X	X
E6	X	X	X			X
E7	X	X	X			X
M3	X			X	X	X

	Risk Activities					
Metric Quest	Identification	Strategy / Planning	Assessment	Mitigation/ Avoidance	Reporting	Prediction
M4	X			X	X	X
M5	X		X	X	X	X
M6	X		X	X	X	X
M7	X		X	X	X	X
D2	X			X		X
D3	X		X			X
D5	X			X		X
D6	X			X		X
D7	X		X	X		X
T1	X			X		X
T3	X		X			X
T4	X		X			X
T5	X		X			X
T6	X		X			X
T9	X					X
RC1	X					X
RC2	X					X
RC3	X					X
RC4	X					X
RC5	X					X
RC6	X					X
U2	X					X
C4	X		X	X		X
C5	X		X			X
C7	X		X	X		X
C9	X		X	X		X
R7	X		X			X
R9	X		X	X		X
R10	X		X	X		X
R11	X		X	X		X
R12	X		X	X		X

Questions in the Test Phase

The answers to these metric questions can be used to clarify the impact the six risk management activities have on the test phase of software development. In the following paragraphs, these risks are presented in a series of six steps. Each step builds upon the other. In each step, the risk activity is identified, followed by a list of metric questions that relate to that particular activity.

1. Risk identification: Because this activity affects the test phase and the following phase of the software development life cycle, all of the metric questions specified for the test phase should be considered.
2. Risk strategy and planning: O3, E5, E6, and E7.
3. Risk assessment: O1, O3, O7, O8, E5, E6, E7, M5, M6, M7, D3, D7, T3, T4, T5, T6, C4, C5, C7, C9, R7, R9, R10, R11 and R12.
4. Mitigation/avoidance: O1, O3, O6, O7, O8, E5, M3, M4, M5, M6, M7, D2, D5, D6, D7, T1, C4, C7, R9, R10, R11, and R12.
5. Risk reporting: E5, M3, M4, M5, M6, and M7.
6. Predicting risks: all of the metric questions applicable to the test phase should be used so that future risks are avoided.

Purpose

The purpose of this step is to help you generate the SERIM metrics required to calculate your project's risk in the TEST phase of development. You can then examine the risk metrics applicable to each of the six risk management activities, identify specific areas of risk derived from the metric questions, and develop action plans to manage these risks.

Delivery and Maintenance

The delivery and maintenance phase includes logging and completing customer problems, enhancing the software with new features, and delivering adequate help information for the user. Since decisions made at this phase of the software life cycle affect the customer, the risk impacts of the decisions reflect on the organization's ability to satisfy the customer. One thing that I have observed again and again in software project development is that old code never dies; it grows into the next release. The risks associated with maintaining existing code pose a different set of circumstances than those involved with development of new code. The economics of software reuse is the main driving force in these circumstances.

Software reuse of code is driven by predicted effort (costs) and time-to-delivery (schedule) pressures. We have all heard many times that it is less costly to write good software once than to continue to use difficult software over and over. Nevertheless, old software is usually abandoned only when new hardware technology is introduced, creating a chance to write the software over again. With this in mind, the following JIT approaches apply.

Besides reusing code, reuse the regression test suite developed during the testing phase. Update the test suite when problems are fixed or new functionality has been added. Prototype or model significant changes before they are implemented. Like initial software development, understand the risks before they are implemented.

Although keeping design documentation up to date is very useful, unless it is used for training someone later, it is expensive and time consuming. The old design should be filed away in a library with new design documentation made for only major enhancements to the software product.

To help measure risks associated with the delivery and maintenance phase, the following table contains the software risk metric questions that should be considered.

Identification of Risk Activities Against Metric Questions in the Delivery and Maintenance Phase.

Metric Quest	Risk Activities					
	Identification	Strategy / Planning	Assessment	Mitigation/ Avoidance	Reporting	Prediction
O1	X		X	X		X
O2	X	X	X	X		X
O3	X					X
O4	X					X
O5	X			X		X

Metric Quest	Risk Activities					
	Identification	Strategy / Planning	Assessment	Mitigation/ Avoidance	Reporting	Prediction
O6	X		X	X		X
O7	X		X	X		X
O8	X	X	X	X	X	X
E6	X	X	X			X
E7	X	X	X			X
M3	X			X	X	X
M4	X			X	X	X
M5	X		X	X	X	X
M6	X		X	X	X	X
M7	X		X	X	X	X
D2	X			X		X
D3	X		X			X
D6	X			X		X
T1	X			X		X
T6	X		X			X
T7	X		X			X
T9	X					X
RC1	X					X
RC2	X					X
RC3	X					X
RC4	X					X
RC5	X					X
RC6	X					X
U1	X					X
U2	X					X
C5	X		X			X
C8	X		X	X		X
R8	X		X	X		X

Questions in the Delivery and Maintenance Phase

The answers to these questions can be used to clarify the impact the six risk management activities have on the delivery and maintenance phase of software development. In the following paragraphs, these risks are presented in a series of six steps. Each step builds upon the other. In each step, the risk activity is identified, followed by a list of metric questions that relate to that particular activity.

1. Risk identification: Identifies risks affecting the delivery and maintenance phase of the software development life cycle. All of the metric questions pertaining to this phase should be considered.
2. Risk strategy and planning: O3, E5, E6, and E7.
3. Risk assessment: O1, O3, O7, O8, E5, E6, E7, M5, M6, M7, D3, T6, T7, C5, C8, and R8.
4. Mitigation/avoidance: O1, O3, O6, O7, O8, E5, M3, M4, M5, M6, M7, D2, D6, T1, and R8.
5. Risk reporting: E5, M3, M4, M5, M6, and M7.
6. Risk prediction: All of the metric questions that apply to the delivery and maintenance phase should be used to prevent future problems associated with risks.

Purpose

The purpose of this step is to help you generate the SERIM metrics required to calculate your project's risk in the DELIVERY AND MAINTENANCE phase of development. You can then examine the risk metrics applicable to each of the six risk management activities, identify specific areas of risk derived from the metric questions, and develop action plans to manage these risks.

Action Plans

Recognizing the Need for an Action Plan

Consider the following points as you "drill down" through the levels in any of the five analytical perspectives to the individual metric questions. The presence of one or more of these conditions should alert you to the need to develop an action plan to resolve issues and problems.

3. An individual low score (below 5)
4. A significant drop in score
5. A downward trend in scores, even if current score is above 5

Actions

Actions are specific, proactive steps taken by the project manager or project team to resolve the issues and problems underlying problematic scores for any particular SERIM metric question. The goal of actions should be to raise the score for the metric question.

Action Plan Name

You will need to enter a name for each action plan you create.

Actions Needed

Enter the specific actions you plan to take to raise the score of the metric question you have selected. The actions you choose to take may be based on

1. your own past experience regarding interventions that work (or don't work).
2. the experience of team members and others within your organization regarding interventions that work (or don't work).
3. research contained in recent professional journal articles and books.
4.   the resources of the IEEE Computer Society.
5. recent information on the SERIM Customers' Private Web site.
6. any combination of the above.

Resources Needed

When writing your action plan, consider the following four categories of resources as potential sources of help in resolving software development problems.

Information Resources

Consultation support from people outside the team (specify names and type of help needed from each person). Consultants may be available within or outside the organization.

Communication Resources

*   Improved communication between sponsoring organizations (specify how)
*   Improved communication within the project team (specify how)
*   Improved communication between the project team and senior management (specify how)

- Improved communication between the project team and other project teams (specify how)

Human Resources
- More people assigned to the project (specify number)
- A different mix of people assigned to the project (specify names)
- More experienced people assigned to the project (specify names)

Material Resources
- More money (specify amounts, areas of budget, and supportive rationale)
- Additional/different equipment (specify number and type of hardware/software)
- Adjustment of timeline for project schedule (specify deadlines/ milestones to be adjusted, and how these adjustments will be made)

Who is Responsible?
The names of the project team members who will implement, complete, and follow up on the action plan.

Entered
The date the action plan for a particular metric question was written. The application will enter this date automatically. The date entered by the application is "read only." No adjustments are possible.

Implemented Target
The projected date for implementing the action plan.

Implemented Actual
The date the action plan is actually implemented.

Completed Target
The projected date for completing the action plan, and resolving the issues and problems underlying low scores.

Completed Actual
The date the action plan is actually completed and issues resolved.

SUPPORTING SERIM: Getting Help

There are four ways to get help with the Software Engineering Risk Management application.
1. The Smart Help System™ within the application.
2. This Reference Guide
3. Technical Support from LearnerFirst via e-mail.
4. SERIM Customers' Private Web Site

Smart Help System™

LearnerFirst's Smart Help System is an embedded system that provides immediate access to helpful support information, assistance, and guidance, wherever you are working in the application. Smart Help gives you the benefit of Dr. Karolak's best thinking on the subject of Software Engineering Risk Management, in the amount you choose, at the time you choose. All of the on-line information contained in the Smart Help System is also available in print within this Reference Guide. To access Smart Help, follow these instructions.

Instructions
1. Click on the Help icon at any point in the application, or

2. Click on HELP in the Top Toolbar, or

3. Press the F1 key. A help screen related to your current area of work will appear.

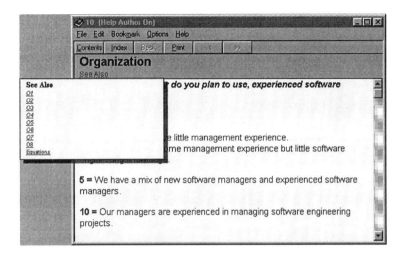

4. Click on the buttons in the Help Toolbar to navigate within the Smart Help System, as described below.

Contents	Displays a list of the available help topics.
Back	Returns to the last topic you viewed.
Index	Searches for topics by keywords.
Underline	Jumps to a related help topic. Click on the green underlined words.
Dotted Underline	Displays definition. Click on green dotted underlined words to see a definition of the word. Click again to dismiss the definition.

LearnerFirst E-mail Support

Our e-mail address is **lfsupport@learnerfirst.com**

Be sure to include the information listed below, so that we can respond quickly to your questions.
1. Name
2. Company name
3. Phone #

4. Describe the problem, suggested enhancement, or question. Please be as detailed and specific as possible.
5. Where in the application did this problem occur? State the Step name found in the title bar.
6. What were you doing?
7. What can we do to help?

SERIM Customers' Private Web Site

LearnerFirst maintains a private, password-protected web site for SERIM customers. On this site, you will find pertinent articles, discussions of risk-related topics, links to additional resources, and new application updates for you to download.

Instructions
1. Type this URL address in your browser:

    www.learnerfirst.com/serim/

    The Enter Network Password dialog box will appear.

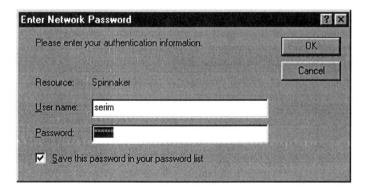

2. Enter **serim** in the User Name data entry box.
3. Enter **serim3** in the Password data entry box. The SERIM Customers' Private Web Site will appear. Follow the directions on the screen to navigate within the web site.

WORKING WITH SERIM: Examples

Three sample projects have been included with your Software Engineering Risk Management application. Each project is located in the installation directory with the extension **.srm**.

To view one of these projects, select FILE Open from the Top Toolbar. You will see the file names for the three examples in the list box.

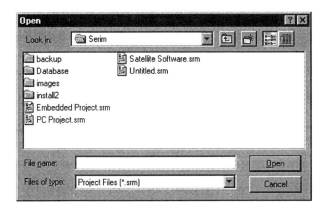

- **Embedded Project.srm** - Embedded software that will provide signal processing and control for electronic steering.
- **PC Project.srm** - Software system to be delivered during a 24 month period. It will be comprised of commercial and customized software totaling approximately 25,000 lines of Ada and C code.
- **Satellite Software.srm**- Software used to test a satellite system prior to its being used in a space environment.

Example 1 - Satellite Software Project

Suppose we have a collection of software used to test a satellite system prior to its being used in a space environment. It is written in 200,000+ lines of a higher level language and has stringent real-time data collection requirements. It resides on several mini-computer systems and includes many advanced mathematical techniques for its reporting capability. Most of the software is custom written for the data collection applications, but some commercial software is used for data reporting applications. The software is interfaced to gather data from several different types of test equipment which involve multiple types of data conversion, buffering, and timing requirements to interface with the test equipment and the mini-computers. The software development environment uses standard vendor-based tools for compiling and debugging. The development schedule varies based on the different tests that must be performed but ranges from one week to six months. Since most of the software has been released to the customer, the project is in the delivery and maintenance phase of the software life cycle. Using SERIM, responses to the metrics questions appear in the following table.

See the risk metric ratings and interpreting the results for the Satellite Software Project.

Satellite Software Project - Risk Metric Question Ratings

Metric ID	Rating	Metric ID	Rating	Metric ID	Rating
O1	10	T1	10	C1	8
O2	9	T2	6	C2	5
O3	10	T3	5	C3	3
O4	10	T4	0	C4	5
O5	8	T5	0	C5	8
O6	8	T6	0	C6	5
O7	10	T7	0	C7	3
O8	10	T8	10	C8	7
E1	6	T	10	C99	10
E2	0	RC1	10	R1	9
E3	10	RC2	10	R2	9

Metric ID	Rating	Metric ID	Rating	Metric ID	Rating
E4	10	RC3	10	R3	9
E5	10	RC4	8	R4	9
E6	7	RC5	8	R5	*
E7	8	RC6	9	R6	6
M1	6	RC7	8	R7	4
M2	5	RC8	8	R8	10
M3	8	RC9	8	R9	0
M4	5	RC10	2	R10	3
M5	10	RC11	0	R11	3
M	10	U1	3	R12	0
M7	10	U2	5	P1	10
D1	9	U3	5	P2	10
D2	10	U4	10	P3	10
D3	7	U5	10	P4	10
D4	6	U6	8	P5	10
D5	5				
D6	10				
D7	5				

Satellite Software Project - Probability Assessment

Probability Subtree	Risk	Probability Subtree	Risk
Overall	7.42	Pre-Requirements	8.00
Technical	7.09	Requirements	8.44
Cost	7.59	Design	8.41
Schedule	7.59	Coding	8.29
Organization	9.38	Testing	6.95
Estimation	7.29	Delivery and Maintenance	8.15
Monitoring	7.71	Risk Identification	7.01
Development Methodology	7.43	Risk Strategy and Planning	7.17
Tools	4.56	Risk Assessment	6.38
Risk Culture	7.36	Risk Mitigation and Avoidance	6.88
Usability	6.83	Risk Reporting	8.29
Correctness	6.00	Risk Prediction	7.01
Reliability	5.64	Process	7.45
Personnel	10.00	Product	7.09

Satellite Software Project - Interpreting Results

Now let us review the data and interpret its meaning. The probability of success for the project is 7.40. This means that the project's risk between 0 (the worst) and 10 (the best) scored 7.40 based on answers to the risk questions. The three lowest probabilities for success (viewing the project from its probability subtrees) are the risk factors tools at 4.60, reliability at 5.60, and correctness with a probability value of 6.00.

The low probability value for success for the software risk factor tools is based on responses to a series of questions addressing the use of automated testing tools. The probability value conveys the testing function is projected to be very laborious because of the lack of automated tools, and if the schedule is tight, it may not test all the needed functionality. Since this project is in its maintenance phase, the lack of regression test tools poses the risk of introducing new bugs into the software without testing for changes that may affect current functioning software.

Example 2 - PC Project

The PC Project is a software system that is to be delivered during a 24-month period. It will be comprised of commercial and customized software totaling approximately 25,000 lines of Ada and C code. Highlights of the requirements identify the target environment consisting of personal computer platforms and other microprocessor-based hardware. The software product is graphic, database-oriented and used for radio frequency communication planning. Its real-time requirements include interfacing to various types of communication devices (such as radios used for secure communications) and filling them with information that will allow these devices to exchange data. The displays and printed reports are required to have a dual language capability. The software development environment consists of state-of-the-art PC-based tools. Four releases of the software are planned over the 24-month period. The project is in the requirement phase of the software life cycle.

PC Project - Risk Metric Question Ratings

Metric ID	Rating	Metric ID	Rating	Metric ID	Rating
O1	7	T1	5	C1	9
O2	7	T2	8	C2	*
O3	5	T3	5	C3	*
O4	8	T4	3	C4	*
O5	6	T5	0	C5	8
O6	9	T6	10	C6	*
O7	10	T7	*	C7	*
O8	7	T8	8	C8	*
E1	7	T9	7	C9	*
E2	10	RC1	8	R1	*
E3	8	RC2	8	R2	10
E4	10	RC3	4	R3	*
E5	10	RC4	2	R4	10
E6	7	RC5	2	R5	*
E7	8	RC6	1	R6	*
M1	10	RC7	7	R7	*
M2	8	RC8	8	R8	*

Metric ID	Rating	Metric ID	Rating	Metric ID	Rating
M3	8	RC9	6	R9	*
M4	8	RC10	5	R10	*
M5	10	RC11	0	R11	*
M6	10	U1	10	R12	0
M7	5	U2	10	P1	7
D1	7	U3	10	P2	3
D2	8	U4	7	P3	5
D3	7	U5	0	P4	4
D4	10	U6	10	P5	10
D5	10				
D6	10				
D7	4				

PC Project - Probability Assessment

Probability Subtree	Risk	Probability Subtree	Risk
Overall	6.55	Pre-Requirements	6.45
Technical	6.08	Requirements	6.18
Cost	6.79	Design	6.65
Schedule	6.79	Coding	6.91
Organization	7.38	Testing	6.06
Estimation	8.57	Delivery and Maintenance	6.16
Monitoring	8.43	Risk Identification	6.23
Development Methodology	8.00	Risk Strategy and Planning	7.42
Tools	4.63	Risk Assessment	6.38
Risk Culture	4.64	Risk Mitigation and Avoidance	6.76
Usability	1.83	Risk Reporting	8.43
Correctness	8.50	Risk Prediction	6.23
Reliability	6.67	Process	6.61
Personnel	5.80	Product	5.95

PC Project - Interpreting Results

There are several observations that can be made about the data presented for each of the projects to provide a valid comparison. For the PC project, the probability of success for the project is 7.00. Given that a perfect score is 10 and the worst score is 0, this represents a very good probability of success at this point in the software development life cycle. The three lowest probabilities for success, viewing the project from its subtrees, are the risk factors: risk culture at 4.60, tools and personnel with probability values of 5.80. In order to understand why these factors scored as they did, you did some additional investigation, which resulted in the following findings.

The low probability value for success when addressing the software risk factor risk culture is based on responses to a series of questions addressing trade-offs among risks and technical performance, cost, and schedule, along with the lack of a risk management practice. The probability value indicates willingness to make risk trade-offs affecting budget, schedule, and technical performance without a formal assessment of the risk involved. This approach to risk management is inherently less effective and has a lower probability of success.

Responses to a series of questions addressing the use of automated testing tools and staff training to use the tools yielded a low probability value for the success of the risk factor of tools. The probability value indicates the testing function is projected to be very laborious because of the lack of automated tools, and if the schedule is tight, it may not test all the needed functionality that should be tested. This risk is compounded by the low indication of the skill level of the software engineers based on their training using the tools.

The low probability value for success with the software personnel risk factor is based on responses to questions addressing experience of the personnel related to product type, development environment, and implementation language. The probability value indicates new personnel who are unfamiliar with the project and/or product type. This may influence the software development schedule and budget, while the new personnel work through the learning curves in each of these areas. Even though these areas have more potential risk, there is still time in the project to plan to decrease the risk in these areas and improve the score.

Example 3 - Embedded Project

The Embedded Project provides an example of embedded software that will provide signal processing and control for electronic steering. The software is microprocessor-controlled on customized electronics, runs real-time, and is highly coupled with the hardware. Some of the requirements identify that the software must control an electric motor's speed, as well as monitor and adjust the motor's current consumption based on control signals and feedback from the motor circuitry. Memory and processing speed are limited by the microprocessor selection; this is a constraint in the design of the software. There are approximately 6,000 lines of assembly code and tight execution time limits required. The software development environment consists of workstation-based tools for design, compile, link, unit test, and emulators for hardware/software debugging. The schedule for this project is 12 months, and the project is currently in the coding phase of the software life cycle.

Embedded Project - Risk Metric Question Ratings

Metric ID	Rating	Metric ID	Rating	Metric ID	Rating
O1	8	T1	9	C1	5
O2	10	T2	8	C2	4
O3	6	T3	4	C3	3
O4	7	T4	0	C4	2
O5	5	T5	0	C5	3
O6	5	T6	0	C6	4
O7	8	T7	*	C7	0
O8	7	T8	5	C8	*
E1	7	T9	4	C9	*
E2	0	RC1	10	R1	9
E3	6	RC2	10	R2	9
E4	8	RC3	8	R3	8
E5	10	RC4	4	R4	10
E6	0	RC5	8	R5	10
E7	0	RC6	10	R6	6
M1	10	RC7	7	R7	10
M2	3	RC8	8	R8	10

Metric ID	Rating	Metric ID	Rating	Metric ID	Rating
M3	6	RC9	8	R9	0
M4	5	RC10	8	R10	*
M5	10	RC11	0	R11	*
M6	7	U1	*	R12	0
M7	7	U2	*	P1	5
D1	5	U3	0	P2	7
D2	7	U4	10	P3	7
D3	5	U5	8	P4	7
D4	7	U6	6	P5	10
D5	4				
D6	8				
D7	3				

Embedded Project - Probability Assessment

Probability Subtree	Risk	Probability Subtree	Risk
Overall	5.93	Pre-Requirements	6.20
Technical	5.90	Requirements	6.21
Cost	5.95	Design	6.70
Schedule	5.95	Coding	6.53
Organization	7.00	Testing	5.26
Estimation	4.43	Delivery and Maintenance	6.45
Monitoring	6.86	Risk Identification	5.92
Development Methodology	5.57	Risk Strategy and Planning	4.75
Tools	3.75	Risk Assessment	5.17
Risk Culture	7.36	Risk Mitigation and Avoidance	5.47
Usability	6.00	Risk Reporting	6.86
Correctness	3.00	Risk Prediction	5.92
Reliability	7.20	Process	5.92
Personnel	7.20	Product	5.91

Embedded Project - Interpreting Results

The probability of success for the Embedded project is 5.80. This is a low score considering the project is in the coding phase. The three lowest probabilities for success, viewing the project from its subtrees, are the risk factors correctness at 3.00, estimation at 3.50, and tools with a probability value of 3.80.

The low probability value for correctness is based on responses to questions indicative of the process of identifying all the software requirements and the traceability of software. The probability value indicates that in the coding phase, there are major risks of not implementing all the requirements into the software product.

Estimation has a low probability value for success. This value is based on responses to a series of questions associated with cost modeling and past estimating experience. The probability value indicates past estimates, estimating methods, and historical data used have not been accurate enough to predict future cost and schedule. Based on these past results, it is not likely that future estimates will be accurate.

The low probability value for the success of the risk factor tools is based on responses to questions addressing the use of automated testing tools, tool stability, and tool availability. The probability value indicates the testing function is projected to be very laborious because of the lack of automated tools. If the schedule is tight, this may not test all the needed functionality. Problems may occur due to incorrect software operations with unstable tools, and resource contention, such as personnel and testing tools, may exist. All of these activities may also affect the project budget.

Based on these results, you deduce that the additional effort of tracing software requirements to the software, using a better estimation method, and acquiring and using test tools would help raise the probability of success for this project.

LEARNING ABOUT SERIM: Underlying Principles

Dr. Dale Karolak

The Problem

Do I even need to say it? There is a problem out there with software development! Within the last twenty years, the cost of developing software has exceeded the cost of developing the hardware platforms it executes on [14]. During that time frame, the software technology effectiveness, that is, the cost-performance ratio, for computer-based systems has increased at a rate of 1000 every 10 years [15], resulting in the movement of additional functionality from hardware to software. Over the last 30 years, software technology has seen six orders of magnitude increase in performance-price gain [16]. Today, it is estimated that over 90 percent of computer system costs are associated with software [17], and that software development and maintenance represents an industry cost of over $300 billion a year [18].

Despite the economic and functional importance of software, developing software is still generally thought of as a high-risk effort, and little progress has been made in improving the management of these risks. One example illustrating the lack of software risk management is the perception that an overwhelming majority of the problems with late deliveries of software are related to software technology problems (such as the development of complex algorithms), over which there is little control. Research negates this perception, and shows that 45 percent of all causes for delayed software deliveries are organization-related problems which management can control [19].

The lack of successful software management has contributed to the realization and fulfillment that software development is an uncontrolled activity that is not being managed in an effective manner. From a business viewpoint, the success criteria used to measure software development efforts include return on investment, time to market, and customer satisfaction. From a technology viewpoint, the success criteria used to measure software development efforts include meeting functional requirements, usability of the product, and future support. Based on a survey conducted by the United States General Accounting Office, the results of software development efforts and the management of the risks using these success criteria are not too impressive. In this survey, 50.4 percent of the vendors supplying software to the United States Government indicated that software development is associated with cost overruns, and 62 percent indicated that software development is also associated with schedule overruns [20]. A similar study performed in the United Kingdom (one that involved 60 companies and more than 200 software projects) indicated that 55 percent had experienced cost overruns, and 66 percent also experienced schedule slippages [21].

The Industrial Viewpoint

Software management can be viewed from two macro perspectives: an industrial view and a practitioner view. The industrial view sets an overall picture of how software development process efforts, and their associated risks, relate to software products. The practitioner's view influences the activities, or lack of, performed during software development that relate to the project's success. Both of these views independently contribute to the symptoms of poor software management: that is, late deliveries, budget overages, and erroneous or missing technical performance expectations.

Although there are several problems associated with software development, the industrial viewpoint targets the three most prevalent ones:

1. The perception that the production of software is still not recognized as a major development effort. As identified previously, 90 percent of all computer system costs is associated with software. Most companies developing software, especially software embedded in hardware platforms, track the identity and associated project costs with the delivered end item, which in most cases, is hardware. The inability to identify software costs occurs because it is buried into the cost account for the hardware product. This happens when the *Work Breakdown Structure* (WBS) is not organized to identify software development as a separate item. In more recent times, major corporations developing software have recognized this and are keeping better cost data. For software being developed by medium- and smaller-sized companies, however, software development is still often not recognized as a major development effort.

2. Despite many advances in software engineering as a discipline since it was first defined in 1968 [22], there is still the perception that software is a creative endeavor—that it cannot be "engineered" like other disciplines. One Air Force decision-maker made this observation: "You software guys are too much like the weavers in the story about the Emperor and his new clothes. When I go out to check on a software development the answers I get sound like, 'We're fantastically busy weaving this magic cloth. Just wait a while and it'll look terrific.' But there's nothing I can see or touch, no numbers I can relate to, no way to pick up signals that things aren't really all that great. And there are too many people I know who have come out at the end wearing a bunch of expensive rags or nothing at all" [23]. Inconsistent application and management of the software engineering discipline still contribute to this perception.

3. The perception that even if it is recognized that software development contains risk, nothing can be done to control the risks. History has shown most software endeavors are late, over budget, and have poor or missing technical performance. This assertion has been documented in many research findings, including research by Suding [24], which shows that the typical software development project is 47.5 percent over budget. In another study, Dinitto states that in some extremes, cost growth can reach 1000 percent [25]. Putnam states the typical software development project is 200–300 percent over budget and 100 percent over schedule [26]. In a study of five large software telecommunications projects, Karolak found software projects were up to 158 percent over budget and 89 percent over schedule [27]. Other examples from industry include data on cost overruns and schedule slippages from Allstate Insurance, The City of Richman, Business Men's Assurance, and Blue Cross & Blue Shield United of Wisconsin [28]. Davis [29], using government data, demonstrated that out of nine software projects funded by the U.S. Government, 29 percent of the software costs was spent on software that was never delivered, and another 19 percent contained errors and missing requirements that needed extensive rework. Davis determined that only 2 percent of the total costs in the study were spent for software that initially met the customer requirements and was used without modification as shown in the following figure.

The Practitioner Viewpoint

From a practitioner viewpoint, there are several problems associated with the risks of software development. The four most prevalent ones are:

1. *The lack of understanding/education of what is involved in the management of software*. The concept of software development management and the risks involved in this type of product are not readily addressed in our university educational system or commercial training seminars. Management concepts can be found in university business programs, which only occasionally addresses the concept of risk as it relates to investment or insurance decisions. However, these concepts are not easy to associate with the software engineering process.

2. *The lack of discipline when implementing good management techniques*. Even if one is educated in good software management practices and risk management techniques, it requires much rigor and discipline to identify, calculate, determine, plan, collect, and report software risk items. It can be a laborious task, especially when one is constrained by budget and schedule pressures.

3. *The lack of tools needed to perform software risk management*. Although more project management tools are currently being made available for software project management, the tools to implement a software risk management program are not well identified, not automated, not easily accessible, and not available to most software professionals. If the tools are not readily available and easy to use, software management techniques that consider risks will not be performed.

4. *The limited view of software management and the lack of integrating software management initiatives*. Little information associated with software risk management has been identified in specific areas during the software development life cycle, such as cost estimation or testing. Thus, most people who have been introduced to the activities of software risk management have a limited view of when, what, and how it can be performed. To be more effective, software risk management must be viewed holistically throughout the software development life cycle.

The Example

So what does this mean to you? Let us see if the following scenario sounds familiar. You are a software manager leading a software project that is twelve months into an eighteen month software development cycle in which the software developers are coding and performing some unit testing. You are already four weeks behind schedule, but you are not too worried because you will figure some way to make up the time because of a slow start getting the project off the ground. The software development team is in good spirits.

Now it is month sixteen. You are supposed to be well into integration testing. You have started some integration but many software modules are still behind schedule. As a matter of fact, your overall schedule is now estimated to be seven weeks behind. You are working the software developers overtime hoping to catch up on the schedule but that has not worked. Your budget for the project has been overrun, and you are expecting a significant cost growth. You have used all of your hours saved under management contingency. Your management is worried. You are worried. But you hope that a plan, one that is based on all the time you spent in reviews and updating documents, will pay off in the end because of less errors during testing.

It is month eighteen. You have not completed integration. You are still continuing to find software bugs. This is a fixed-price job. The projection for any profit is lost. The company is eating the cost. Pressure to ship the software increases, but the software does not meet the requirements. You hear the following comments: "The problems are in the software, not the hardware"; "The software is late again, as usual"; and "Those software people can never meet a schedule or a budget!" You are asked when the software will be completed. Best projections are two more months. The customer is upset because their product will not be shipped to them on time. You sit down and call your lead software developers together. As a team, you reflect on what you did. You followed the software engineering procedures that took over a year to develop and train. Those procedures were even audited by an outside agency. You wrote the specifications, documented the designs, held the reviews, developed test plans and procedures, and your estimates where based on the software developers and your best judgments. Sure you took some shortcuts, but nothing significant. It was not good enough.

So what is wrong? Is it the people? Is it the tools? Is it the process? The answer in most cases is more than likely a combination of all of the above. So what do you do? Give up hope?

The Example (Continued)

Let us explore some general areas. First, the people. The people involved in software development fall within two categories: the developers and the supports (including management). I truly believe the statement made by Boehm: the biggest influence on most projects is the quality of the people who work on it [17]. This gives you two choices as a software project manager: beg, borrow, steal, or hire the best software developers you can find, or, take what you have and use them. Needless to say, the latter is what happens in most cases. Given that is the case for most of us, and that we are content (or have no choice) with the norm, let us move on and discuss management.

In my opinion, management is the best candidate for having the most influence on the project. Management sets the overall direction, makes the major decisions, and should be ultimately responsible for the outcome of the project. Besides, it is easier to replace an individual or two in management than a whole development team. If our jobs were based on the results of delivering a high-quality product on time and within budget, most software managers would have been unemployed a long time ago. Assuming that our senior managers (based on past experience) cannot expect any better from us, and since they seem unwilling to fire us yet, most of us are given many chances to try to improve our management skills on the next software project. Let us assume that management is constantly looking for a way to improve meeting the concerns of the customers and their businesses.

What About Tools?

You will probably always be lagging in the tool race. By the time you think you have the best tools to do the job, there are new ones that will make the ones you have obsolete. That does not mean that you should stop trying; you need to keep up with what you have and improve upon it to help increase your productivity and quality of the software. If you do not, your competition will.

Finally, let us discuss the process. The process used expends most of the energy and money in the software engineering field (this is where most consultants make their money). What process should you be following? *Structure design? Object-oriented? Cleanroom?* The choices are not easy and, in many cases, are not made based on the perceived benefits and problems for the project. I have found that no matter which process is used, it tends to be sequential and stills follows the waterfall process, that is, requirements, design, code, and test. In general, there is nothing wrong with this process. Most people understand this process and feel comfortable with it. It is within the context of the process that I find the answer to the question raised in the example given at the end of Section 1: that is, "what is wrong with this?"

In the example, the product (software) was not able to be completed within the expectations of time, schedule, and quality, even though the process was followed, assuming good management complemented an acceptable software development team, and adequate tools were given to do the job. Would it have helped if the team had used a different development methodology? Maybe. But I have found in most cases that management and the supporting methodology do not support identifying risks in the software development process and project. It is here that those unexpected problems, rework, and addition of late resources causes the best planned schedules and budgets to be overrun.

Software is an intellectual activity, therefore it is difficult to manage. Since most people do not think exactly in the same terms, there tends to be problems communicating requirements and directions, integrating software, and finding and fixing problems. How these unknowns are addressed in the future constitutes risk.

The problem most software development methodologies experience is that they do not address risk, such as identifying project risks and acting on them. Without the knowledge of risk management concepts which are inherent in the software development process, the ability to identify, plan, assess, mitigate, report, and predict risks is almost impossible. Addressing these risk management activities will change the perceptions of them, thus reducing the symptoms associated with poor software risk management.

Territories, Maps, and Bridges

Software development risks are currently viewed from two major perspectives: the technological and the business viewpoint. The technological perspective identifies the tools, techniques, and implementation environment of the software. The business perspective addresses resources, schedules, and business impact (which measure software in terms of business success). These two perspectives may be thought of as different views, or maps, that address the territory of software risk management.

These views are separately categorized. The technology map is the main concern of the software manager; while the business map is the main concern of the senior level management. When *software developers or their managers define software risk*, it is in terms of technology. Likewise, when defined by senior management in the company, it is in terms of performance and profit.

These maps are usually exclusive of each other, but in some cases they overlap. Neither completely encompasses the entire territory of software risk management as it is defined. The different maps viewed in the perspective of business and technology must become integrated to effectively address the issues of software risk management.

Cost and schedule concerns may be addressed in a business perspective. In many cases, however, software risk management is not addressed from a strategic business perspective. It is my premise that strategic and operational risks are differentiated in the development of software, and that they must relate to each other. Also, risk management should be structured across the software development life cycle in order to implement a risk management approach that meets overall business concerns.

The integrated map cannot occur without a bridge that links the two perspectives together and encompasses the unknown software risk territories. The way the bridge can be built is based on three concepts: software risk management education/awareness, methodology, and tools.

A holistic software risk management methodology addressing the software development life cycle from a business and technology perspective, combined with a software risk management tool, is necessary to build this bridge. More on this topic later.

Just-In-Time Philosophy and Strategy

Software *Just-In-Time* (JIT) has its philosophical basis in JIT manufacturing. JIT manufacturing is based on the concept that inventory is reduced, thereby diminishing carrying charges and overhead expense [30]. This in turn reduces material lot sizes, set-up time, and results in a reduced cycle time with a product that has less cost associated with it. The opposite of JIT is *Just-In-Case* (JIC), stockpiling extra reserves of material in case there is a problem. The results of JIT manufacturing has been documented over several decades of practice, and has now established itself as the norm for competitive manufacturing practices.

JIT software is a management risk-driven approach to developing software. JIT software addresses the following concepts:
1. risks (instead of inventory) and their contingencies built into the software process should be minimized
2. management of risks early in the development process will reduce cycle time
3. risk management will result in a product that has less cost associated with it, and has a better chance in meeting schedule commitments.

There are many activities and costs associated with activities related to poor software risk management. The most notable of these is what practitioners refer to as *fire fighting*, late deliveries, and product delivered with poor quality and/or reduced functionality. The equivalent examples of JIC in software that relate to risk contingencies include inflated estimates in development effort, schedules that do not meet customer expectations by padding with extra months because of anticipated risks, and a product that does not satisfy the customer requirements based on expected, but unplanned for, changes during development.

The identification of risks and its management throughout the software development life-cycle is the cornerstone of JIT software. With any good management approach, planning is key to a successful beginning of a project.

Plan, Plan, Then Re-Plan

Just like a good inventory control system is critical for JIT manufacturing, good planning is essential for JIT software. Planning for change is a part of good planning. Software planning should encompass how to get through tomorrow, while taking into account the overall business perspective.

Depending on the type of software (whether it is a product itself or part of a product), strategic planning should take place. Considerations for strategic planning involve the needs, features, and strategies for a product line and its evolution. As a result of this type of planning, a written *vision statement* should be produced that gives a general sense of direction for the product line that should be built into the software. The results of strategic planning, such as a vision statement, are then incorporated into the requirements of the software, such as expendability, flexibility, or maintainability considerations.

Current ABC Products

| Product 1 | | Product 2 | | Product 3 | | Electronics Display Controls |

Vision Statement: The family of ABC products will be expanded into the new markets of electronic display controls over the next five years.

Future Software Requirements for ABC Products: The software shall be able to incorporate LCD displays as an option. As an architectural consideration, the use of electronic display controls shall be precluded.

Incorporating Strategic Planning Concepts Into Software Requirements

Future ABC Products in New Market

Electronics Display Controls

| Product 1 | Product 2 | Product 3 |

Operational planning is associated with the day-to-day project planning that addresses cost, resources, and schedule. The foundation of operational planning (that is, how to get from where you are in the project to its completion), is known as the tool *Program Evaluation and Review Technique* (PERT) [31] diagram. PERT diagrams have been in use for the last three decades, but have not been exploited as a tool for software management. The PERT diagram shows a visual road map detailing the necessary steps for completing the software task. The advantages of using the PERT diagram versus other types of schedule and planning tools are:

1. It identifies all major activities. Each major activity is identified as a PERT item.
2. Each PERT item abstraction can then be further defined into other subtasks.
3. With each PERT item, a start date, completion date, description of the task, and personnel assignment can be identified.

4. Estimates on the amount of effort can be associated with each PERT item.
5. Probabilities of completion or risk identifiers can be identified.
6. Dependencies between activities are identified in a PERT diagram. This is one of the most attractive features of using a PERT.
7. From the above information, calculating the longest path to completion through the PERT network can identify the critical path.

PERT diagrams are a powerful method of controlling and helping to identify future consequences of decisions made in the present. An example of a simple PERT diagram for software requirements through coding phases is shown in the following figure.

Identify Risks Early

Knowing that you will use a PERT as your means to plan the software project and identify the steps, each PERT activity can then be associated with a Work Breakdown Station (WBS). Now let us discuss some strategies that will influence the best way to draw up the PERT diagram.

JIT software is concerned with risk, therefore your PERT diagram must reflect activities that identify risks early in the software life cycle. The basic premise of JIT software is to find the unknowns as soon as you can in order to manage the process better, make adjustments to resources to accommodate the risks, and make better cost and schedule estimates.

There are some well-proven methods for identifying risks early. One of these methods is reviewing. Reviews have their biggest payoff if performed early in the life cycle (such as concept and requirements reviews), and before the product is produced. I am not convinced that code reviews give you great risk reduction benefit for the effort expended.

Other types of activities involved in JIT software which help identify risk earlier are prototyping, cumulative partition software acceptance, and the arrangement of software builds based on minimal acceptance criteria.

Develop in Parallel

In order to have a managed approach to problems instead of a reactionary approach, start tasks as soon as possible to identify potential future risks. Most software project and software development methodologies suggest completing a task before you move on; the JIT software approach runs counter to this idea and requires parallel development.

Parallel development is not an easy task to manage—this is another reason for the use of PERTs. *Parallel development* means staffing the software project with more people early in the software development cycle and also completing the project earlier (this goes along with the saying that time is money).

Let me give a small example of parallel software development activities. During the requirements phase, a requirements statement is generated to identify software functionality. Usually, errors associated with the definition and implementation of the functionality are found during unit or integration testing. Sometimes you are lucky and find some of them in a review. To identify risks early (the risks of implementing wrong functionality), implement a requirements document, while simultaneously generating a prototype of user functionality (person–machine interfaces and reports). The parallel development of the requirements document and the prototype then become the requirements for the software to be developed.

So what does JIT software do to the cost and schedule of development? I contend that JIT software reduces costs and schedules mainly because the investment involved in identifying risks early results in a managed approach to solving problems. This costs less and takes less effort than finding the same problems later in the development life cycle and then reworking efforts which have already been expended (it costs more to feed the marching army).

More On Software Risk Management and Just-In-Time

Since JIT concepts are risk based, why have these concepts not been fully explored before? The topic of software risk management has mainly been viewed from the operational aspects of developing software, that is, the concerns of risk from an implementation, day-to-day perspective by researchers. Risk must be addressed not only from a project viewpoint, but also from a collective view of a business entity.

Risk Management Perspectives

Although these operational views are important, risk management must take on some, if not all, of the characteristics of the business enterprise and the risks the enterprise will accept. Managers of software in-the-large (or that of many projects) must consider a wider range of risks than software in-the-small (or a single project). From this premise, I have defined JIT and risk management from strategic and operational perspectives. The following figure illustrates this point and shows example risk concerns from both the strategic and the operational perspective.

Strategic risk management identifies risks and creates plans of strategic (or future) importance to the business enterprise. Recognition that exists apart from the day-to-day operations of the business is vital to performing strategic risk management. For example, the relationship between risk and profit recognizes that in a purely competitive economic system, profits would disappear if it were not for uncertainty and risk. Profit and risk must coexist, or economic enterprise would cease to exist. Likewise, strategies involving business plans must also be concerned with risk.

From a strategic business perspective, risk involves viewing the business enterprise as a whole, as well as the possible consequences, actions, and results that can result from future decisions.

In the world of enterprise, the following areas involve some type of risk: property and personnel, marketing, financial, personnel and production, and environment. With software risk management, strategic risks consist of only three areas: market risk, financial risk, and personnel and production risk.

Software market risks revolve around the uncertainty of capturing, expanding, or generating a market share with respect to the software product (these three aspects are highlighted in the following examples.) The introduction of Lotus 123™ for spreadsheet applications is an example of capturing a software market. This software captured the market from inferior products and set a standard for electronic spreadsheets. Microsoft has proven itself very adept at expanding an existing market, and software such as Word™ for word processing applications, Mail ™ for electronic mail capabilities, and Project™ for project management planning has expanded Microsoft's market beyond DOS. The Harvard Graphics™ product generated market share by creating a market for visual representation of data. In each case, the risks of these products involved an up-front capital investment with an unknown return on investment.

Financial risks involve the uncertainty of an investment's return of a profit or of a loss. Since risk and profit are directly related, the amount of financial investment in software versus the return on investment based on future returns must be considered. Since software tends to add value (such as more functionality, features, and flexibility to products) without adding much size, weight, and power consumption, the financial investment of future market share, sales, and profit must be weighed against the perceived risks associated with software. These perceived risks include not completing the software task on schedule, exceeding the budget, and producing a product that does not meet the customers' needs.

Personnel and production risks involve the ability to produce a high-quality product in a timely manner, with the available resources. *High quality* refers to meeting the customers' expectations about the software use and functionality. *Timely manner* is the ability to capture the market share and meet consumers' demands before they purchase an alternative product. Together, quality and timeliness represent risks determined by the customer purchasing the software product.

As defined by Hedges [32], *strategic risks* can also be classified according to loss severity. There are three classifications of severity:
- **Class I:** Those losses that do not disturb a firm's basic finances.
- **Class II:** Those losses that would require borrowing or selling new common stock.
- **Class III:** Those losses larger than Class I or II, which might bankrupt the firm.

Examples of strategic software risks in Class I loss severity include minor losses such as late delivery without market impact, a minor software problem with a product, or going over budget and reducing the profit margin. The late introduction of Windows NT™ into the PC market is an example of a Class I loss severity.

Risks associated with Class II loss severity necessitate obtaining increased capital to recover from losses. Examples of this include cancellation of a project or product line, fire or significant damage to the facilities, or major outstanding debts due to litigation such as experienced by Lotus and Borland corporations over their respective spreadsheet products.

Examples of strategic software risks in Class III loss severity include all of the Class II examples (on a broader scale), with additional examples including missing market windows (the right product at the wrong time), and producing products that are of poor quality or do not meet customer needs (the wrong product at the right time). Several *Computer Aided Design* (CAD) software packages that did not survive the market shakeup fall within this class.

Strategic risk decisions must be reflected in an operational sense in order to maximize the overall strategic objectives. Without the flow-down of strategic risk decisions to operational actions, strategic decisions will not be carried out. In the case of software, strategic decisions take the form of technology (leader or follower), types of software products (embedded or applications), business expertise (development, support, or integrator), or market segment.

Operational Risk Management

In terms of the business view, *operational risk management* involves identifying risks and important plans that affect the daily operation (operation and the development of a product) of the business enterprise. From a business perspective, Mehr and Hedges [33] briefly describe the risks associated with continuity of operations with respect to pre-loss and post-loss objectives. Henley and Kumamoto [34] identify examples of operational risk management concerning hardware products and reliability. Shumskas [4] describes the concepts from a customer point of view as the risk incurred for continued software development from the contractor.

The operational business perspective of risk involves viewing the project or task and the possible consequences, actions, and results that can be made based on future decisions. Operational risks relate to only a segment of the business enterprise. Examples of operational risks include cost, schedule, and technical performance of the software product.

Cost risk exists for the following reasons:
1. Based on today's competitive environment, long-term budgets are rarely fixed.
2. The project is competing for monies and resources with other programs and investment alternatives.
3. In 90 percent of the cases, the true cost of software development is underestimated in the beginning of the project [34].
4. In most cases, the software product to be developed is not completely identified when it is estimated.
5. There is never enough good historical data upon which to base the next project.

Since this environment is not unusual, there is significant cost risk associated with developing software.

Schedule risk exists because of factors that are related to the development effort. These factors include personnel, tools, and hardware dependencies. The Personnel risk factor contributes to schedule risk, since people work at different productivity rates. Personnel also affect the hours spent on a project because of the amount of time needed to understand the computer language or tools used. Software development and test tools have similar results. Depending on the type and ease of use, tools can accomplish a task much quicker than tasks performed manually. Hardware dependency risk factors include the response time, the development hardware availability and access, and the availability of the target hardware for system test and integration.

Technical risk occurs because of several reasons, including the introduction of new technology in a product, the pioneering of new technology, and the lack of information concerning what needs to be done or what can be done. Examples of software development technical risk include the use of a new language (introduction of new technology), the application of parallel processing and logic programming to embedded space applications (pioneering of new technology), the design of user–machine interfaces without customer feedback (lack of information of what needs to be done), and the development of software not knowing whether critical timing parameters can be met (lack of information of what can be done).

Operational risk decisions are also a function of risk determinants [12]. There are three risk determinants: lack of control, lack of information, and lack of time. Risks associated with lack of control are events that cannot be influenced, such as a computer breakdown during final testing. Risks related to lack of information include unknown bugs in a compiler, the amount of time the software needs to be tested, and the effectiveness of the software reviews held. Risks associated with lack of time include the completeness of the software tests, the quality of the design considerations and alternatives, and the amount of functionality incorporated into the design. The amount of risk taken based on these three determinants is shown in the following figure.

In order to minimize the failure of the project, the operational risks presented must be identified in the project process. Risk considerations must be made in order to manage the software development project properly. Just-In-Time software identifies these risks and provides a framework methodology to manage a software project. To view these risks and to provide the framework, elements of software risk must first be identified.

RESEARCHING SERIM: References

[1]   Rowe, W.D., *Anatomy of Risk*, Krieger Pub. Co., Malabar, 1988.

[2]   McCall, J.A., P.K. Richards, and G.F. Walters, "Factors In Software Quality," General Electric Command and Information Systems, Tech. Report 77DIS02, Sunnyvale, 1977.

[3]   Boehm, B.W., J.R. Brown, H. Casper, M. Lipow, G.L. MacLeod, and M.J. Merrit, *Characteristics of Software Quality*, North Holland, 1978.

[4]   Shumskas, A.F., "Software Risk Management," *Proc. NSIA Conf. on Software Risk Management*, 1989.

[5]   Cooper, L., "DoD Policies and Standards for Software Risk Management," *Proc. NSIA Conf. Software Risk Management*, 1987.

[6]   Holloway, C.A., *Decision Making Under Uncertainty: Models and Choices*, Prentice-Hall, Englewood Cliffs, N.J., 1979.

[7]   Greene, M.R. and O.N. Serbein, *Risk Management: Text and Cases*, Reston Publishing Co., Reston, 1978.

[8]   Boehm, B.W. and N.P. Papaccio, "Understanding and Controlling Software Costs," *IEEE Trans. Software Eng.,* Vol. 14, No. 10, Oct. 1988.

[9]   Brooks, F.P., *The Mythical Man-Month*, Addison Wesley, Reading, Mass., 1975.

[10]   Griffiths, R.F., *Dealing With Risk—The Planning, Management, and Acceptability of Technology Risk*, Wiley & Sons, New York, 1981.

[11]   Augustine, N.R., *Augustine Laws*, American Institute of Aeronautics and Astronautics, New York, 1983.

[12]   MacCrimmon, K.R. and D.A. Wehrung, *The Management of Uncertainty Taking Risks,* The Free Press, New York, 1986.

[13]   Bicknell, K.D. and B.A. Bicknell, *Quality Function Deployment*, CRC Press, Cleveland, 1994.

[14]   Boehm, B.W., "Software Engineering Economics," *IEEE Trans. Software Eng.,* Vol. SE-10, No. 1, Jan. 1984.

[15]   Musa, J.D., "Software Engineering: The Future of a Profession," *IEEE Software,* Vol. 2, No. 1 Jan. 1985.

[16]   Brooks, F.P., Jr., "No Silver Bullet: Essence And Accidents of Software Engineering," *Computer,* Vol. 19, No. 4, Apr. 1987.

[17]   Boehm, B.W., *Software Engineering Economics*, Prentice-Hall, Englewood Cliffs, N.J., 1981.

[18]   Martin, J. and C. McClure, *Software Maintenance: The Problem and its Solution,* Prentice-Hall, Englewood Cliffs, N.J., 1983.

[19]   van Genuchten, M., "Why Is Software Late? An Empirical Study of the Reasons for Delay in Software Development," *IEEE Trans. Software Eng.,* Vol. 17, No. 6, June 1991.

[20]   United States Accounting, "Comptroller General Report to the Congress of The United States," Report no. FGMSD-30-4.

[21]   Putnam, L.H. and D.T. Putnam, "Software Investment Management," *Proc. IEEE/AIAA 7th Digital Avionics Conf.*, 1986.

[22]   Naur, P. and B. Randell, eds., "Software Engineering," NATO Scientific Affairs Division, Brussels, 1969.

[23]   Boehm, B.W., "Software and its Impact: A Quantitative Assessment," *Datamation*, May 1973.

[24]   Suding, A.D., "Hobbits, Dwarfs, and Software," *Datamation*, July 1977.

[25]   Dinitto, S.A. Jr., "Software Engineering Problems And Progress," *J. Electronic Defense*, Vol. 9, No. 8, Aug. 1986.

[26]   Putnam, L.A., *Software Cost Estimating and Life-Cycle Control: Getting the Software Numbers,* IEEE Computer Society Press, Los Alamitos, Calif., 1980.

[27]   Karolak, D.W., "Software Cost Estimation: Problems of Yesterday and Promises for the Future," Masters Thesis, University of Phoenix, 1985.

[28]   Rothfeder, J., "It's Late, Costly, Incompetent—But Try Firing A Computer System," *Business Week,* Nov. 7, 1988.

[29]   Davis, A.M, *Software Requirements Analysis & Specification*, Prentice-Hall, Englewood Cliffs, N.J., 1990.

[30]   Schonberger, R.J., *Japanese Manufacturing Techniques—Nine Hidden Lessons in Simplicity,* The Free Press, New York, 1982.

[31]   Wiest, J.D. and F.K. Levy, *A Management Guide To PERT/CPM*, Prentice-Hall, Englewood Cliffs, N.J., 1977.

[32]   Hedges, B.A., "Proper Limits in Liability Insurance: A Problem in Decision Making Under Uncertainty," *J. Insurance*, Vol. 28, No. 2, June 1961.

[33]   Mehr, R.L. and B.A. Hedges, *Risk Management, Concepts, And Applications*, Richard D. Irwin Inc., Homewood, 1974.

[34]   Henley, E.J. and H. Kumamoto, *Probabilistic Risk Assessment*, IEEE Press, New York, 1992.

MORE ABOUT SERIM: Additional Readings

Charette, R.N, *Applications Strategies for Risk Analysis*, McGraw-Hill, New York, 1989.

Crockford, N., *An Introduction to Risk Management*, Woodhead-Faulkner, Cambridge, 1980.

Crossman, T.D., "Software Quality in the Fourth-Generation Technique Environment," *Data Processing,* Vol. 25, No. 10, Dec. 1985.

Grechenig, T. and S. Biffl, "Making Code Metrics Useful For Practioners," *Proc. 3rd Software Engineering Research Forum*, 1993.

Karolak, D.W., "Identifying Software Quality Metrics For A Large Software Development," *Proc. IEEE Global Telecommunications Conf.*, 1985.

Karolak, D.W. and J. Zschernitz, "An Applied Methodology in Software Defect Prevention," *Proc. Nat'l NSIA Software Conf.*, 1989.

Lawler, R.W., "System Perspective on Software Quality," *Proc. 5th Int'l Computer and Applications Conf.* (COMPSAC), IEEE Computer Society Press, Los Alamitos, Calif., 1981.

Lawrence, W.W., *Of Acceptable Risk: Science and the Determination of Safety*, William Kaufman, Los Altos, Calif., 1976.

Murine, G.E., "Applying Software Quality Metric," *Proc. ASQC Congress Trans.,* Boston, 1983.

Singleton, W.T. and J. Hovden, *Risk and Decisions*, Wiley & Sons, New York, 1987.

Sommerville, I., *Software Engineering,* 3rd ed., Addison Wesley, Reading, Mass., 1989.

Taul, G., "Quality Factors and Support Risk," *Proc. NSIA Conf. Software Risk Management,* 1987.

——, "A New Deming Experience—Japan's Software Assault," *Proc. ASQC Congress Trans.*, 1986.

——, "Integrating Software Quality Metrics With Software QA," *Quality Progress*, Nov. 1988.

INVESTIGATING SERIM: Equations

Overall Project Risk

$P(A) = [\sum_{n=1}^{3} P(An)]/3$ assuming that each risk element is equal in weight. If the weight of each element differs between them, then $P(A) = w1P(A1) + w2P(A2) + w3P(A3)$ where each wi is a positive number and $w1 + w2 + w3 = 1$.

Technical

$P(A1) = [\sum_{n=4}^{13} wnP(An)]$ where $w4 = 0.043$, $w5 = 0.043$, $w6 = 0.087$, $w7 = 0.087$, $w8 = 0.087$, $w9 = 0.13$, $w10 = 0.13$, $w11 = 0.13$, $w12 = 0.13$, $w13 = 0.13$ Based on Figure 9-2, a weight of 0.043 was assigned for a low value, 0.087 for a medium value, and 0.13 for a high value.

Cost

$P(A2) = [\sum_{n=4}^{13} wnP(An)]$ where $w4 = 0.136$, $w5 = 0.136$, $w6 = 0.136$, $w7 = 0.136$, $w8 = 0.09$, $w9 = 0.09$, $w10 = 0.045$, $w11 = 0.045$, $w12 = 0.045$, $w13 = 0.136$. Based on Figure 6-2, a weight of 0.045 is assigned for a low value, 0.09 for a medium value, and 0.136 for a high value.

Schedule

$P(A3) = [\sum_{n=4}^{13} wnP(An)]$ where $w4 = 0.136$, $w5 = 0.136$, $w6 = 0.136$, $w7 = 0.136$, $w8 = 0.09$, $w9 = 0.09$, $w10 = 0.045$, $w11 = 0.045$, $w12 = 0.045$, $w13 = 0.136$. Based on Figure 6-2, a weight of 0.045 is assigned for a low value, 0.09 for a medium value, and 0.136 for a high value.

Organization

$P(A4) = [\sum_{n=1}^{8} (On)]/8$ where On is the metric value for the question number On.

Estimation

$P(A5) = [\sum_{n=1}^{7} (En)]/7$ where En is the metric value for the question number En.

Monitoring

$P(A6) = [\sum_{n=1}^{7} (Mn)]/7$ where Mn is the metric value for the question number Mn.

Development Methodology

$P(A7) = [\sum_{n=1}^{7} (Dn)]/7$ where Dn is the metric value for the question number Dn.

Tools

$P(A8) = [\sum_{n=1}^{9} (Tn)]/9$ where Tn is the metric value for the question number Tn.

Risk Culture

$P(A9) = [\sum_{n=1}^{11} (RCn)]/11$ where Rcn is the metric value for the question number Rcn.

Usability

$P(A10) = [\sum_{n=1}^{6} (Un)]/6$ where Un is the metric value for the question number Un.

Correctness

$P(A11) = [\sum_{n=1}^{9} (Cn)]/9$ where Cn is the metric value for the question number Cn.

Reliability

$P(A12) = [\sum_{n=1}^{12} (Rn)]/12$ where Rn is the metric value for the question number Rn.

Personnel

$P(A13) = [\sum_{n=1}^{6} (Pn)]/6$ where Pn is the metric value for the question number Pn.

Pre-Requirements

$P(A14) = S(O1, O2, O3, O4, O5, E1, E2, E3, E4, E6, E7, M1, M2, M3, M4, M6, M7, D1, D2, D6, T1, T6, T9, RC1, RC2, RC3, RC4, RC5, RC6, RC7, RC8, RC9, RC10, RC11, C5, P1, P2, P3, P4, P5)/40$

Requirements

P(A15) = S(O1, O3, O4, O5, O6, O7, O8, E5, E6, E7, M3, M4, M5, M6, M7, D2, D3, D4, D6, T1, T6, T9, RC1, RC2, RC3, RC4, RC5, RC6, U2, U3, U5, C1, C5, R3)/34

Design

P(A16) = S(O1, O3, O4, O5, O6, O7, O8, E5, E6, E7, M3, M4, M5, M6, M7, D2, D3, D4, D6, T1, T2, T6, T9, RC1, RC2, RC3, RC4, RC5, RC6, U2, U4, U6, C2, C5, R1, R2, R3, R5)/38

Coding

P(A17) = S(O1, O3, O4, O5, O6, O7, O8, E5, E6, E7, M3, M4, M5, M6, M7, D2, D3, D4, D6, T1, T6, T8, T9, RC1, RC2, RC3, RC4, RC5, RC6, U2, C3, C5, C6, R1, R2, R3, R4, R5, R6)/39

Testing

P(A18) = S(O1, O3, O4, O5, O6, O7, O8, E5, E6, E7, M3, M4, M5, M6, M7, D2, D3, D5, D6, D7, T1, T3, T4, T5, T6, T9, RC1, RC2, RC3, RC4, RC5, RC6, U2, C4, C5, C7, C9, R7, R9, R10, R11, R12)/42

Delivery and Maintenance

P(A19) = S(O1, O3, O4, O5, O6, O7, O8, E5, E6, E7, M3, M4, M5, M6, M7, D2, D3, D6, T1, T6, T7, T9, RC1, RC2, RC3, RC4, RC5, RC6, U1, U2, C5, C8, R8)/33

Risk Identification

P(A20) = ($\sum_{n=1}^{81}$ Qn)/81 where Qn is a metric question from the set of (O1 - O8, E1 - E7, M1 - M7, D1 - D7, T1 - T9, RC1 - RC11, U1 - U6, C1 - C9, R1 - R12, P1 - P5)

Risk Strategy and Planning

P(A21) = S(O3, E1, E2, E3, E4, E5, E6, E7, M1, D1, RC11, P1)/12

Risk Assessment

P(A22) = S(O1, O2, O3, O7, O8, E2, E3, E4, E5, E6, E7, M5, M6, M7, D3, D7,
T2, T3, T4, T5, T6, T7, U3, U4, U6, C1, C2, C3, C4, C5, C6, C7, C8, C9,
R1, R3, R4, R5, R6, R7, R8, R9, R10, R11, R12, P1)/46

Risk Mitigation and Avoidance

P(A23) = S(O1, O3, O6, O7, O8, E2, E3, E4, E5, M1, M2, M3, M4, M5, M6,
M7, D1, D2, D4, D5, D6, D7, T1, RC10, RC11, U3, U5, C1, C2, C3, C4,
C6, C7, R8, R9, R10, R11, R12, P1, P2, P3, P4)/42

Risk Reporting

P(A24) = S(E5, M2, M3, M4, M5, M6, M7)/7

Risk Prediction

P(A25) = $(\sum_{n=1}^{81} Qn)/81$ where Qn is a metric question from the set of (O1 - O8,
E1 - E7, M1 - M7, D1 - D7, T1 - T9, RC1 - RC11, U1 - U6, C1 - C9, R1 -
R12, P1 - P5)

Process

P(A26) = $[\sum_{n=4}^{13} wnP(An)]$ where w4 = 0.125, w5 = 0.125, w6 = 0.125, w7 =
0.125, w8 = 0.125, w9 = 0.125, w10 = 0.04, w11 = 0.04, w12 = 0.04, w13
= 0.125. Based on Figure 6-3, a weight of 0.04 is assigned for a minor
influence and a value of 0.125 was assigned for a major influence.

Product

P(A27) = $[\sum_{n=4}^{13} wnP(An)]$ where w4 = 0.045, w5 = 0.045, w6 = 0.045, w7 =
0.045, w8 = 0.14, w9 = 0.14, w10 = 0.14, w11 = 0.14, w12 = 0.14, w13 =
0.14. Based on Figure 6-3, a weight of 0.045 is assigned for a minor
influence and a value of 0.14 is assigned for a major influence.

CUSTOMIZING SERIM: Request Form

Does your organization need a customized version of SERIM? Take advantage of LearnerFirst's ability to design a version of this application specifically to meet your needs. Please consider the questions below, then contact us at **lfsupport@learnerfirst.com** for a detailed discussion of your objectives, time frame, and budget.

Do you want to:

1. Add your organization's logo?

2. Change the Main Screen?

3. Change the operating environment?
   - LAN
   - Web
   - Both

4. Change the wording in the Application steps?

5. Change the methodology (add or remove steps or metric questions)?

6. Other customized changes? (Please list)

APPENDIX A: List of SERIM Metric Questions

ID	METRIC QUESTION
O1	Are you using or do you plan to use experienced software managers?
O2	Has your company produced software similar to this in the past?
O3	Is a documented organizational structure in place or planned which accurately describes communication channels and lines of authority?
O4	Will the organization's structure remain stable during the project life cycle?
O5	What is the confidence level of your management team regarding the organization's ability to deliver the software product on time, on or below budget, and with high quality?
O6	Do good communications exist between different organizations supporting the development of the software project?
O7	Are software configuration management functions being performed?
O8	Are software quality functions being performed?
E1	What estimation method is used?
E2	Is a software cost model used that accurately estimates project cost?
E3	Is the cost estimate based on past software productivity metrics?
E4	Are the schedule estimates based on the schedules of past software projects?
E5	Are estimates revised on a monthly basis or less?
E6	How closely do your past cost estimates correlate with actual project cost?
E7	How closely do your past schedule estimates correlate with actual project schedules?
M1	Are distinct milestones set for every development phase of each major software project?
M2	Is a detailed WBS used to track and report costs and budget for each piece of major software development?
M3	Is there a monitoring system setup to track cost, schedule, and earned-value?
M4	Are cost, schedule, and earned-value reports available on demand?
M5	Are cost, schedule, and earned-value reports updated on a monthly basis, or more frequently?
M6	Is there a problem or action log system that is used and updated on a weekly basis?
M7	Is there a process for addressing and recording technical problems that is used and updated weekly?
D1	Is there a documented software development methodology/plan for the project that is closely followed?

ID	METRIC QUESTION
D2	Are the software developers trained in the software development methodology?
D3	How closely is the software development methodology followed?
D4	Does the software development methodology include requirements, design, and code reviews/walkthroughs/inspections?
D5	Does the software development methodology require test plans and/or test procedures for all software functions?
D6	Does the software development methodology require documentation, such as requirements, design, and software development folders?
D7	Is software regression testing performed?
T1	Are the software developers trained to use the software tools identified for the project?
T2	Are automated tools used for software design?
T3	Are automated tools used for software testing?
T4	Are automated tools used for software test procedure generation?
T5	Are automated tools used for software regression testing?
T6	Are automated tools used for software requirements traceability?
T7	Are automated tools used for software re-engineering (identifying existing characteristics of the software based on its code, such as its structure, data dictionary, etc.)?
T8	How stable is your compiler/linker/debugger?
T9	Are the software tools required for the project readily available to the software developers when needed?
RC1	Is your company willing to trade increased budget risks for higher profit?
RC2	Is your company willing to trade increased schedule risks for higher profit?
RC3	Is your company willing to trade increased technical risks for higher profit?
RC4	Is your company willing to trade decreased budget risks for lower profit?
RC5	Is your company willing to trade decreased schedule risk for lower profit?
RC6	Is your company willing to trade decreased technical functionality for lower profit?
RC7	Is your company market-driven?
RC8	Is your company's culture conservative in its decision making?
RC9	How would you rate your company's investment in new products and technology?
RC10	Does your company build new products and/or technology in-house, or

ID	METRIC QUESTION
	acquire them?
RC11	Does your company practice and document formalized risk management procedures?
U1	Has the user manual for the software product been developed, tested, and revised?
U2	Are there help functions available for each input or output screen?
U3	Is the user involved in reviewing prototype or early versions of the software?
U4	Is the user interface designed to an industry standard or to a standard familiar to the user?
U5	Have user response times been identified?
U6	Has the design been evaluated to minimize keystrokes and data entry?
C1	Have all the software requirements been identified and documented?
C2	Have software requirements been traced to the design?
C3	Have the software requirements been traced to the code?
C4	Have the software requirements been traced to the test procedures?
C5	Have there been, or do you anticipate, many changes to the software requirements?
C6	Is the software design traceable to the code?
C7	Is the software design traceable to the test procedures?
C8	Have all the open action items been addressed and resolved prior to delivery to the customer?
C9	Has software functional testing been performed prior to customer delivery?
R1	Do error-handling conditions exist for every possible instance within the software design and code?
R2	When an error condition is detected, does processing continue?
R3	Are error tolerances defined for input and output data?
R4	Are inputs checked for valid values before processing begins?
R5	Are hardware faults detected and processed in the software?
R6	Is the use of global data types in the software minimized?
R7	Is defect data collected during software integration?
R8	Is defect data being logged-in and closed-out prior to delivery to the customer?
R9	Is a software reliability model used to predict reliability?
R10	Are test plans used to perform software tests?
R11	Has stress testing been performed?
R12	Does a group separate from the software development group perform software testing?
P1	Are the software personnel resources needed for the project available

ID	METRIC QUESTION
	and identified?
P2	How experienced are the software personnel resources in the product type being developed?
P3	How experienced are the software personnel resources in the software development environment?
P4	How experienced are the software personnel resources in the software implementation language?
P5	Have an adequate number of personnel been assigned for the peak of the project?

APPENDIX B: SERIM Keystroke Combinations

COMMAND	MNEMONIC ACCESS
FILE	Alt + F
New	Alt + F, N
Open	Alt + F, O
Save	Alt + F, S
Save As	Alt + F, A
Print	Alt + F, P
Print Setup	Alt + F, R
Exit	Alt + F, X
EDIT	Alt + E
Cut	Alt + E, T
Copy	Alt + E, C
Paste	Alt + E, P
STEPS	Alt + S
Project Description	Alt + S, D
Project Assessment	Alt + S, A
• Organization	Alt + S, A, O
• Estimation	Alt + S, A, E
• Monitoring	Alt + S, A, M
• Development Methodology	Alt + S, A, D
• Tools	Alt + S, A, T
• Risk Culture	Alt + S, A, R
• Usability	Alt + S, A, U
• Correctness	Alt + S, A, C
• Reliability	Alt + S, A, L
• Personnel	Alt + S, A, P
Analytical Perspectives	Alt + S, P
• Risk Elements	Alt + S, P, E
• Risk Factors	Alt + S, P, F
• Risk Categories	Alt + S, P, C
• Development Phases	Alt + S, P, D
• Risk Activities	Alt + S, P, A
Next	Alt + S, N
Previous	Alt + S, R
INTRO	Alt + I
Navigation	Alt + I, N
Software Engineering Risk Management	Alt + I, S

COMMAND	MNEMONIC ACCESS
WINDOW	Alt + W
Tile	Alt + W, T
Cascade	Alt + W, C
Arrange All	Alt + W, A
HELP	Alt + H
Contents	Alt + H, C
Search for Help On	Alt + H, S
About	Alt + H, A

IEEE

COMPUTER SOCIETY

Press Activities Board

IEEE Computer Society Publications

The world-renowned Computer Society publishes, promotes, and distributes a wide variety of authoritative computer science and engineering texts. These books are available in two formats: 100 percent original material by authors preeminent in their field who focus on relevant topics and cutting-edge research, and reprint collections consisting of carefully selected groups of previously published papers with accompanying original introductory and explanatory text.

Submission of proposals: For guidelines and information on Computer Society books, send e-mail to cs.books@computer.org or write to the Acquisitions Editor, IEEE Computer Society, P.O. Box 3014, 10662 Los Vaqueros Circle, Los Alamitos, CA 90720-1314. Telephone +1 714-821-8380. FAX +1 714-761-1784.

IEEE Computer Society Proceedings

The Computer Society also produces and actively promotes the proceedings of more than 130 acclaimed international conferences each year in multimedia formats that include hard and softcover books, CD-ROMs, videos, and on-line publications.

For information on Computer Society proceedings, send e-mail to cs.books@computer.org or write to Proceedings, IEEE Computer Society, P.O. Box 3014, 10662 Los Vaqueros Circle, Los Alamitos, CA 90720-1314. Telephone +1 714-821-8380. FAX +1 714-761-1784.

Additional information regarding the Computer Society, conferences and proceedings, CD-ROMs, videos, and books can also be accessed from our web site at http://computer.org/cspress

4/15/97